MINING
FOR
MEANING

Harvesting Rich Veins of Meaning
from Our Relationships with God, One Another,
and Nature

James D. Bailiff

WORKBOOK PRESS LLC
187 E Warm Springs Rd,
Suite B285, Las Vegas, NV 89119, USA

Website:https://workbookpress.com/
Hotline:1-888-818-4856
Email:admin@workbookpress.com

Ordering Information:
Quantity sales. Special discounts are available on quantity purchases by corporations, associations, and others.
For details, contact the publisher at the address above.

Library of Congress Control Number:
ISBN-13:   978-1-957618-86-9 (Paperback Version)
             978-1-957618-87-6 (Digital Version)

REV. DATE: 01/03/2022

MINING

FOR

MEANING

Harvesting Rich Veins of Meaning from Our Relationships with God, One Another, and Nature

By

James D. Bailiff

DEDICATION PAGE

To my late parents, Joe and Clarice, my beloved wife, Beverly, and our sons, James, Scott, Richard, Douglas, and Michael, and daughter, Cheryl

CONTENTS

Preface...i-vii

Chapter One:

   Our Relationship with God.....................................1-37

Chapter Two:

   Our Relationship with One Another..........................38-59

Chapter Three:

   Our Relationship with Nature.................................60-83

Chapter Four:

   Some Key Dynamics of

   Our Relationships and

   Tools for Mining Them...84-106

Conclusion...107-111

Epilogue..112-113

Notes...114-117

PREFACE

It seems that a strong sense of purpose and meaning is not a widespread experience these days. Rather, compulsion to survive propels us toward rigid routines that aim to control, leaving victims with that "caught-in-a-revolving-door" feeling.

In this book, I am making the case that life has the potential to bathe us in meaning that is able to defy the effects of routines which are working to capture and enslave us. Moreover, I am contending that life calls us to explore its remarkable contents which constitute a veritable mine brimming with rich veins of meaning. But this mine has to be worked and the richness of its veins extracted, refined and applied, a demanding process which requires our strong commitment.

The late Thomas Merton wrote prolifically about the meaning of life. While affirming its availability, he saw the practical difficulty of tapping into it. In the prologue to his book, *No Man Is an Island*, he writes:

> *Our life, as individual persons and as members of a perplexed and struggling race, provokes us with the evidence that it must have meaning. Part of the meaning still escapes us. Yet our purpose in life is to discover this meaning and live according to it. We have, therefore, something to live for. The process of living, of growing up, and becoming a person, is precisely the gradually increasing awareness of what that something is. This is a difficult task for many reasons. 1*

I suspect that choosing to read this book indicates your desire, not for a shallow and routinized existence, but for a fuller life rooted in and sustained by a deeper sense of meaning and purpose. Most likely you are willing to meet whatever the circumstances demand of you in order to discover and experience that deeper quality.

From time to time, all of us may become entangled in webs of meaningless routines, but few of us are content to settle there. We have a desire for something more than a limited robot-like existence. I'm betting that you are willing to stretch yourself to make that dream become a reality.

Where does one start in the journey of discovering meaning? In what context does one find meaning? Does It lie beyond our own individuality? What role do God, other people, and nature play? These are questions addressed by reflective searchers in a variety of contexts. I have found Victor Frankl's responses to be especially insightful.

As you may know, Dr. Frankl, a Viennese psychiatrist, was imprisoned by the Nazis during the Holocaust. What happened in that seething swamp of misfortune did not defeat him but eventually created a positive revolution in his life and enhanced the effectiveness of his work. His vision and desire for something better drove him not only to survive the experience but, in the process, led him to test a theory that resulted in a fresh approach to psychoanalysis and psychotherapy. He learned that human beings who seek meaning under the ordinary living conditions of everyday life became more keenly active in achieving that goal under the extraordinary conditions of harsh, life-threatening imprisonment.

In his close observation of fellow prisoners, Frankl learned that while many of them settled into the routine, most everyone imagined (and longed for) a richer life, and, even under the direst of circumstances, dared to commit themselves to that pursuit.

Two helpful books grew out of his Holocaust experience, *Man's Search for Meaning* and its sequel, *Man's Search for Ultimate Meaning.* In both, Dr. Frankl contends that people are driven, especially under dreadful circumstances, to find meaning. Moreover, he observes that the discovery of that meaning is tied closely to people sharing their mutual suffering with one another and with God.

The discovery of meaning, therefore, is enhanced, not by isolating oneself from others in search of its goal but in moving with others toward it:

> *...man (sic) is originally characterized by his "search for meaning" rather than his "search for himself." The more he forgets himself—giving himself to a cause or another person—the more human he is. And the more he is immersed and absorbed in something or someone other than himself the more he really becomes himself. 2*

Frankl's insights are both convincing and encouraging. They remind us that humanity is driven by a search for meaning. By banding together in a covenant of sharing, we are moved closer to its discovery while God, the wellspring of meaning, moves toward us to enhance the adventure significantly.

More recently, another author, has addressed the issue. In her book, *Christianity after Religion,* Diana Butler Bass, a fellow at Seabury-Western Theological Seminary, writes: *"We find and know ourselves in relation to our location on a journey and through the relationships that form the web of our lives" 3*

In contrast to Descartes's classical definition o f t he s elf in propositional terms ("I think, therefore I am") Bass focuses upon the self prepositionally. She describes such posture as one of relation to others: "By relating to others, human beings construct themselves." 4

Bass strengthens her position by referencing social psychologist George Herbert Mead who in his *Mind, Self and Society* proposed the following:

The individual experiences himself as such, and directly, but only indirectly, from the particular standpoints of other individual members of the same social group…. The self is not something that exists first and then enters into relationship with others but is, so to speak, an eddy in the social current. 5

Both Frankl and Bass remind us that the search for the meaning of life is not to be found in a direction that leads away from others. Rather, we are called into relationships in which our sharing of life becomes a virtual mine packed with veins of meaning.

Can you identify? If you are a person who has been able to enter into relationships that stretch you beyond self-preoccupation, you know that you are a larger person than you would be had you sunk deeper into self-isolation. And if those relationships have enabled your honest sharing with others, leading you to new levels of adventure and commitment, you have experienced things that have infused and refreshed your life with meaning.

In the wake of all this talk about relationality, you may find yourself asking—What about those times I need to be alone? Neither Frankl nor Bass discount the value of times when one moves to be in touch with oneself. Both authors express the value of personal space in which to reflect and to meditate. Certainly, Jesus emphasized the value of moving from the noisy crowds to the quiet place. The culprit is not time alone but isolation.

My own experience tells me that I need and enjoy those moments when I can retreat to reflect, contemplate, meditate and rest. But, so often, these moments are filled with memories and reflections of my relationships with those I love and value. Thus, my alone times become, not an escape into isolation, but an experience of space and quiet that gives me room to consider the nature and value of my relationships and how they may become richer.

Life without significant relationships can leave one lonely, confused, angry and even compulsively destructive. For example, consider Albert Camus' classic novel, *The Stranger*. It's about a young Frenchman by the name of Meursault living in Algiers. The novel presents Meursault as a person who has difficulty establishing meaningful relationships with others. His resulting isolation becomes a source of considerable disappointment and anger which, not only causes him to manipulate and exploit others, but eventually drives him to murder a man who has offended him. For this crime, he is convicted and sentenced to die by the guillotine. As Meursault languishes in his death-row cell, following his ruthless rejection of the prison chaplain's visit, and just hours before his execution, he looks at the night sky, concluding that the universe offers nothing but benign indifference.

Some feel that Camus—a French existentialist—is expressing his own conviction about life's absurdity. Be that as it may, *The Stranger* becomes an effective tool for such commentary and provides readers (whatever their philosophical bent or emotional state may be) with valuable insight into the probability that a life disconnected from positive, life-giving relationships can sink into a disappointing, even catastrophic, absurdity.

Therefore, the approach I have taken in this work reflects commitment to the importance of our relationships as a major source of meaning.

The desire for meaning burns within us and seeks its fulfilment through creative and responsible interface with the key relationships of life—both physical and spiritual—, relationships that constitute life-giving veins of meaning which beg to be mined, processed and applied.

So, in this work I identify what I consider to be the primary relationship categories, namely those which we have with *God, others and nature.* Moreover, I contend that engagement in these relationships, while a natural task may at the same time prove to be an arduous one. To some extent we are already engaged with each one but, given our propensity for focusing too much upon the self, establishing, sustaining and nurturing these relationships constitutes a significant challenge. For example, our relationship with God presents the challenge of discerning the similarity and contrast between God's distinctive nature and our own. It also challenges us at the point of discerning the mind of God and how best, in our human finitude, to relate to such ultimate grandeur. When it comes to our relationship with others, we experience the challenge of balancing our own care with that of others and, identifying the needs of others, how to respond to them appropriately. Then there is our relationship with nature which challenges us to examine where we humans are located within nature's mix, how to relate to its various forces, and whether those respond to us.

Because these key relationships have become somewhat distorted in our imperfect world, their veins of meaning are often heavily covered with cultural debris and, therefore, lie deeply hidden, but ready for our discovery.

In light of that I felt it necessary to identify some tools by which, effectively to engage in mining, tools which will enhance our ability to be successful in fully exposing, extracting, refining and appropriating their potential.

Finally, I contend that, while we may cultivate these relationships to a level at which we draw meaning from them, we do not find completion. I believe that such perfection awaits the finishing touches of God so well symbolized in the great eschatological passages of Scripture, passages in which all creation—already under the work of God's transforming hand—is finally perfected in the coming of *"...a new heaven and new earth"* (Revelation 21:1). This evolving (as opposed to instantaneous) process toward perfection, far from discouraging us in our quest for meaning, is designed to fill us with an expectation that energizes our present efforts, filling us with hope in God's intent for all creation, a hope that daily propels us into giving ourselves to something larger than ourselves.

Thank you for joining me in this exploration of our relationships which are like veins of gold, full and rich, and ready for our mining.

CHAPTER ONE

Our Relationship with God

I believe our relationship with God is foundational for our relationship with others and with nature. For example, in my own experience, the one I have with God affects the value I place upon other human beings and upon nature and, therefore, my approach to them.

This relationship with God is both a simple and complex affair. It's as simple as entrusting oneself to that which surrounds us, transmitting a warmth much like that of a loving parent. Living within that relationship, however, also has its complexity.

The questions we raise in response to that relationship reveal the complexity, questions like these: How can God be everywhere at once? How do I make sense of this mystery? Is God present when experiencing the deep pain common to the journey of life?

I suspect anyone who is building a relationship with God continuously experiences both its simplicity and complexity. It should not be surprising that this relationship generates warmth, and trust, while simultaneously prompting significant questions that may leave one in a relationship accompanied with considerable mystery.

In this chapter I want to share with you something of the character of my relationship with God and insights gained regarding how it continues to bring meaning to me. This relationship with God has the capacity to bless anyone who chooses to enter into it. In the process of our discussion, we will describe ways in which the relationship affects how we perceive God, ourselves, and the world around us.

It is my understanding that everyone's journey into a relationship with God is distinctive. Within the Christian Faith the origin and shape of this relationship reflects human variety. Moreover, not everyone who is in a relationship with God has arrived there by way of the Christian faith. It may be that you have come by one of the other great religions or through no established religion. Indeed, there are varieties of religious experience.

In sharing the personal side of my relationship with God, it is not my intention to present to you an exclusive path, but to share my journey in a way that it becomes inspirational to your own.

In that light, I invite you to join me in exploring the context of my own relationship with God. Perhaps there will be identifiable aspects of this journey, while parts of it may not resonate. Don't be surprised at that, given the fact that there are varieties among us. Uniformity, therefore, is not to be expected in the sharing of our experience.

From a consideration of my religious context, I will proceed to share four important perceptions about God which have served as channels through which meaning flows into my life. Again, you may find aspects in my process identifiable in your own.

Because the nature of my relationship with God is dynamic (versus static), I want to share with you a process in which my perceptions of God continue to evolve from what I consider to be lower perceptions to higher ones. From my own experience, joined to what I have learned from sharing the experience of others, I have discovered a deeper comprehension of God as I move through the different stages of my life. For example, the perceptions I had of God as a child have evolved into richer images as I have grown and developed as a person of faith.

I understand that the ongoing process of our relationship with God is sometimes arrested at a fixed position or diverted in a way that bocks a deeper experience with God. In light of that, I end the chapter by referencing two very dangerously popular and seductive traps which possess the power to damage (if not destroy) a genuinely meaningful relationship with God. These traps lie camouflaged on the road we travel in relating to God and, when tripped upon, severely erode our view of and experience with God.

Now, as promised, let me share some of my own journey in building a relationship with God; then follow by identifying some of the insights of my faith journey which have become channels of meaning.

In a small Appalachian village, I was born into a family that possessed a deep reverence for God. We were connected to a congregation of Christian believers who approached their role in nurturing both the young and the old with considerable seriousness. In that context I began my conscious journey with God, one that has moved with me, through my various phases and continues to bless my life.

As I reflect upon my beginnings, I am increasingly aware of the remarkable people who nurtured me and acted as a conduit to my relationship with God. My mother was instrumental in my becoming involved in all aspects of congregational life—Sunday school, worship, Wednesday night study and prayer meeting, youth groups and marvelous social gatherings which offered great fun, food, and fellowship. As far as my mom was concerned, nothing was to get in the way of our church experience. On the other hand, my dad led me to realize that the arena of God's activity, while including the church, extended beyond. Often, when looking at a beautiful natural scene, he would declare, "Son, the Good Master has made a beautiful world for us!" Moreover, I learned from Dad how important it is to treat others and their property with respect. Even now, when I walk through a store and find a product that has fallen from its shelf, I put it back where it belongs, hearing echoes of Dad's counsel, "Always treat the property of others as responsibly as you treat your own." It was Dad who reinforced the need to treat others (especially the less fortunate) with respect. Rarely did more than a few days pass without Dad reminding my brother and me of the importance of creating life goals and getting a good education with which better to understand and live in the world.

Beyond my parents were all those dear saints who took me under their wing and nurtured me. Mr. Turbyfill and Mrs. Laws were two of my very effective Sunday school teachers who brought to life the Biblical story and helped us youngsters find handles for applying its truth to our lives. Bill Thurmond, a deacon, whom I affectionately called "Uncle Bill", impressed upon me the intensity of God's love. "Son," he would say, "if you were the only person in the world, God would have sent his son just for you." My maternal grandmother (Mamma Lou) led me to see the importance of kindness and hospitality as expressions of our faith while my paternal grandmother (Mammy) taught me the importance of active listening.

It was in such a cradle that my relationship with God was established and nurtured. There, I learned about the warmth of God's love and how to respond to it through both individual and corporate worship. From this faith community, I also learned the blessing of expressing love for God through faithful service to God and to others.

As rich a resource as it was, the community of faith which nurtured my early years had its negative side, too. I witnessed the pseudo-spirituality of self-righteousness, the easy comfort of religious legalism, the arrogance of doctrinal certainty, and the oversimplification of God and godly things. We had our Aunt Rhoda whose self-righteousness could be heard as she looked condescendingly upon modest wine drinking to exclaim, "Well, being a member of the church, you won't catch me drinking that devilish stuff!" We also had Mr. Fields who would warn us frequently not to play "Keeps" (a game played with marbles where a good shooter could win pockets full from the other players) because it was a form of gambling in which Christians should not participate. Then there was Pastor Hall who would proclaim loudly that our particular religious movement was raised up by God to correct the doctrinal mistakes of other religious groups. The trivialization of the Deity could be heard in the admonition of Mrs. Trivett: "Ask God for anything you need and He will give it to you. That's what he's there for!"

For me, however, these negatives were far outweighed by the positives. Even in my youth I could identify some of the fallacies of the negatives and simply slough them off as extreme expressions. The dynamic resource for my own inspiration and growth came from the community's central core of folk whose faith seemed more authentic. It was with that core I would make my connection and feast on its inspiration for worship, fellowship, and service.

This foundational work in building my relationship with God has become an enduring gift. Through every succeeding stage of development into my present "senior hood" I have been sustained and challenged by relating to God's dynamic nature which serves continuously as both a source of peace, and yet, also, discontent.

The peace comes, I believe, from living in the embrace of God's unconditional love. I am not afraid, lonely, estranged, or aimless. A strong sense of purpose and a deep sense of security—like that which is conveyed, theologically, in the Hebrew word, *shalom*, or psychologically in the principle of *homeostasis* (balance) — pulsates within me. I love the way one of the old hymns expresses it: "It is well with my soul."

My relationship with God is also a source of discontent which keeps me from wilting on the vine. Because the relationship is dynamic it keeps me moving, often painfully, from the old to the new. Metaphorically, it's as though God's peace has become a vehicle in which I travel over a curvaceous and bumpy road toward fresh insights and experiences.

I find that traveling this road requires such aids as worship, study, social interaction, and stewardship of resources. I find that, in worship, we are able to act out before God our praise and thanksgiving. From study, we experience new insights that often challenge our existing ones and frequently introduce us to completely new areas for consideration. Prayer, in various forms, sharpens our ability to hear new sounds from God that both inspire and guide. Social interaction (particularly when we expand ourselves beyond the familiar) keeps us in touch with the reality of diversity among people and discourages any retreat into preconceived stereotypes from which we often draw faulty conclusions. Any person who is committed to the stewardship of resources has already heard the call of God to serve in God's vineyard (the world), utilizing the resources God has provided both to honor God and to serve the manifold needs that confront us.

From my relationship with God compelling insights have

emerged which have flooded me with a sense of meaning and purpose. Please allow me to share these and to comment upon each of them briefly:

1. **The Magnetic Dimension of God's Work in Jesus Christ:** I am deeply impressed with the power of God's work in Christ to draw us toward the sacred. Referring to his coming death on the cross, Jesus acknowledged the reality of this divine magnetism when he declared: *"And I, when I am lifted up from the earth, will draw all people to myself"* (John 12:32).

When I contemplate the character of Jesus' life and ministry, all the way to and through the cross, I am deeply moved with a power capable of liberating me from distractions, awakening a sense of being mightily loved, and clarifying my sense of purpose.

A story told during a sermon in Benton Chapel at Vanderbilt University illustrates the magnetic power of God of which I have just spoken. The preacher was The Rev. Dr. Edward Steimle, a Lutheran pastor from New York City and his story continues to inspire me some 50 years later. It's about a young college student so captivated by rationalism and the scientific method that he decides to challenge the religious establishment. He proceeds to a church, asking to see the pastor. Warmly received, he is ushered to the pastor's study where he is greeted by a priest. As soon as they are seated for conversation the young man presents his point: "Sir, I am here to request that you reflect upon your role in contributing to the vast sea of superstition that surrounds us. If you and other clergy will abandon your participation in your religious traditions, society's progress to new levels of intellectual credibility will be enhanced."

The elderly priest listened without interruption. When the young man paused from presenting his case, the priest responded, "I am glad you have come. I hear what you are saying." Without any hint of being defensive, the priest proceeded to ask, "Will you do something for me?" to which the young student responded, "Sir, you have received me warmly and have listened politely. What is it you want of me?"

"Come with me to our place of worship," said the priest.

"Show me the way," replied the student.

Together, they proceeded to the place of corporate worship, a large area surrounded by multicolored stained glass depicting scenes from Jesus' life and ministry.

Everything in the space—the glass, symbols, the shape of the architecture—funneled attention toward a large crucifix hanging above the altar.

For a moment they both stood silent before the scene. Then, the priest made his request. Speaking softly, he asked, "Please go forward, stand at the foot of the steps to the altar, look up at the Crucifix and say, 'Christ died for me.'"

Without any detectable hesitation, the young man agreed and stridently made his way to the area, looked up at the crucifix and declared, "Christ died for me and I don't give a damn!" Returning to the priest, he said, "There it's done."

The priest asked, "Will you please do it again?"

The student returned to the scene, again looked up at the cross and declared, "Christ died for me, and I couldn't care less!"

"Will you do I another time?" the priest asked.

This time the student appeared less strident. As he arrived and looked up, he did not immediately speak; then began to utter haltingly, "Christ…died…for…me…," and then fell to his knees, sobbing.

The priest ran to embrace him. As he took the young man in his arms, he heard him pray, "O God, forgive me. I've been such a fool. I want to yield to your love."

This dramatic story reached deeply into my heart when I heard it years ago. It continues to stir my emotion and sharpen my sense of God's magnetic love. Whether at any given moment my resistance to growth in faith is inordinate pride or despair, the love of God communicating with me through Christ's self-giving nature continues to pull me from the poisonous tentacles of human frailty toward growth, freedom and wholeness.

For several years I have worn a cross around my neck. Occasionally, I reach to feel its presence and to be reminded that love, not hostility or indifference, pulsates at the base of life. The one who knows me best also loves me most. That inspiration gives my life immeasurable meaning.

2. A second insight from my faith that floods my life with meaning comes from an experience and understanding of the work of the Holy Spirit.

The gift of the Holy Spirit is offered to those who entrust themselves to a relationship with God. Their resulting open heart becomes the gate through which the Spirit enters into individuals and corporate bodies, there to become a divine companion, to do the work of spiritual transformation and to offer guidance for the journey of life.

The story of that remarkable Pentecost described in Acts 2 speaks of the coming of the Spirit to Jesus' disciples and of the promise of the Spirit for all who desire the gift.

The initial incident of the Spirit's coming aroused widespread curiosity among the scores of those gathered in Jerusalem from all over the known world, those who had come to the holy city for the important festival. Peter, an apostle, seizes the opportunity to share with them the story of Jesus. Some are so moved by his proclamation that they ask for spiritual direction: *"...what shall we do?"* Peter responds with directions inviting them to repentance and baptism, declaring, *'...and you will receive the gift of the Holy Spirit. For the promise is for you, for your children, and for all who are far away, everyone whom the Lord our God calls to him'"* (Act 2:38,39).

I have received and treasure that gift of the Holy Spirit! Perhaps you have, too. If so, you and I are experiencing three of the most meaningful dimensions of the Spirit's work, companionship with God, transformation of our lives, and divine guidance.

Let's zoom in on spiritual transformation. That work of the Spirit to change us for the better is a beautiful thing. Hear St. Paul speak of it: *"No longer, then, do we judge anyone by human standards.... Anyone who is joined to Christ is a new being, the old is gone, the new has come"* (2 Corinthians 5:16a-17—Today's English Version).

I experience God's Spirit as God taking up residence within me. I sense the same experience in others. And when I share with others, we reach an important consensus that the Spirit has brought us into a process in which, as persons of faith, we are perpetually involved. As we grow in the Spirit, we experience spiritual maturation leading us to become more effective catalysts for positive change in God's wonderful world of creation. As a result, we know that we are more than we used to be and less that what we will become. All of this is accompanied by the realization of a strong sense of purpose and meaning.

Not only do we experience the Spirit's transforming work, but in the midst of it, we become aware of the Spirit's guidance in the midst of life's complexity. Jesus was clear in his reference to such guidance. Intuiting his impending arrest and death, he shared the news with his disciples. Seeing their anxiety at the prospect of losing their leader, he makes this promise regarding continued leadership for them: *"When the Spirit of truth comes, he will guide you into all truth"* (John 16:13—NRSV).

Jesus' promise of the Spirit's guidance does not imply that we are incapable of thinking for ourselves. (I am thankful for the remarkable capacity of the humans to analyze, to weigh options and to make choices. I continue to be impressed with the number of persons who make good choices on a daily basis) Through the Spirit, God enhances our analytic powers and stimulates a sustained process of spiritual transformation, making available, also, a keen capacity for spiritual discernment which promises to yield quality decision making.

So, meaning flows into our lives through openness to the Holy Spirit who brings to us divine companionship, spiritual transformation, and guidance. Does that mean that we don't ever feel lonely or make bad decisions? Of course not! I do think, however, it does mean that our God comes to us even in our loneliness and assures us of acceptance, even when we feel we have erred or failed, giving us confidence to move on.

3. Another insight born on the wings of my faith experience is that God measures our spiritual authenticity by our willingness to do justice.

I am concerned that we tend to measure the authenticity of our relationship with God with inadequate criteria. It seems that more than a few of us use such standards as simply acknowledging God's existence, believing the right doctrines, regular worship attendance, clean language, avoiding scandal, supporting one's family, credit worthiness, managing our anger, paying our bills, etc. While these things have varying degrees of value, none of them is able to bear the burden of serving as the primary criterion for spiritual authenticity.

Perhaps we all know people who give careful attention to some of all of the above standards while, at the same time, appear to tolerate such things as discrimination, poverty and oppression. It is likely that we are able to detect some of that in our own lives, thereby substituting insufficient standards for measuring the authenticity of our relationship with God.

To the extent we are guilty of this substitution, the quality of meaning that flows to us through that relationship may be lowered to a point that we miss the depth implied in Jesus' statement: *"I came that you may have life, and have it abundantly"* (John 10:10—NRSV).

What, then, is a more effective criterion by which to measure the authenticity of our relationship with God? We hear it clearly from the Old Testament prophet, Amos. Although he came from a town in Judah, his message, to mid-8th century B.C.E was to the people of the northern kingdom of Israel.

The problem he addressed was not an absence of religion. Religious observances could be witnessed all over the nation. The problem was their lack of practicing social justice. For example, the prophet discovered that prosperity was limited to the wealthy who were guilty of oppressing the poor. Solution? Amos calls on them to reflect their faithfulness to God by showing justice:

"The Lord says, 'I hate your religious festivals; I cannot stand them! When you bring me burnt offerings, I will not accept them. I will not accept he animals you have fattened to bring me as

offerings. Stop your noisy songs. I do not want to listen to your harps. Instead, let justice flow like a stream, and righteousness like a mighty stream.'" (Amos 5:21-24—TEV).

Similarly, when another prophet, Micah, came to address the southern kingdom of Judah, he found considerable prosperity and power in the hands of a few. In light of such social injustice, he raises the issue of God's requirement:

"God of heaven, when I come to worship him? Shall I bring the best calves to burn as offerings to him? Will the Lord be pleased if I bring his thousands of sheep or endless streams of olive oil? Shall I offer him my first- born child to pay or my sins? No, the Lord has told me what is good. What he requires of us is this: to do what is just, to show constant love, and to live in humble fellowship with God" (Micah 6:6-8).

Centuries later, Jesus showed his reverence for the prophetic tradition by reaffirming its emphasis upon justice. For example, his Sermon on the Mount ((Matthew 5:1-12) precisely calls us to do social justice. His act of cleansing the Temple (Mark 11:15-19) constitutes a protest against injustice. Through his stories, like that of the good Samaritan (Luke 10-29-37), he clearly calls for faith that expresses concern for life's victims.

Our own century is filled with injustice as were the worlds of the prophets and Jesus—racial and gender discrimination, exploitation of the poor, human trafficking, pollution of our environment, political extremism, etc. The prophetic tradition sensitizes modern disciples to authenticate our faith through practicing justice.

Faith's call to justice saves us from the self-righteous temptation to attempt keeping ourselves pure and unstained by separating ourselves from the ugly scenes that injustice creates. In those times, when such separation has been my choice, I have experienced the bumpy noise of hypocrisy staggering, like a drunk person, through the hallways of my soul.

From a faith perspective, working for social justice gives one a sense of relevance, a tangible way to make a difference in the name of God. I shall never forget the evening when my seminary roommate, Clark Ford, and I went out to relax over a game of billiards. It was the fall of 1963 in Nashville, Tennessee, when rigorous efforts were being made by some white businesspersons to keep blacks off their premises.

We arrived at an upscale pool hall of 21st Avenue. The man in charge met us with a smile and we indicated our desire for a table. "Fine," he responded, "just sign this. It doesn't obligate you to anything. It's just our way of being able to keep the damn niggers out of here."

I was momentarily shocked into silence while, Clark, a retired Army sergeant with lots of street smart, quickly responded, "If your intention is to exclude black brothers and sisters from your establishment, we are not interested in playing here!" The manager seemed stunned at such a response from two white southern boys. As we left, I was very thankful that Clark had articulated my own convictions so well. Moreover, I had the sense that our commitment to racial justice represented in our response to the manager's request was the most spiritually authentic thing we had done that day.

Issues of justice continue to confront us. While we have made considerable strides in reducing racial inequality, other issues have surfaced calling for our attention and witness, practical issues such as providing food for the hungry, affordable housing, prison reform, adequate levels for the minimum wage, and immigration laws that leave room for a hospitable compassion and, at the same time, protect a nation from being invaded by those persons and forces intending harm to its citizens.

Wherever there is discrimination or victimization, faith compels us to investigate and take positive action capable of producing positive change. Realizing that doing justice is the authenticating mark of our spiritual commitment, persons of faith are acting on behalf of those who are marginalized. Working for justice in small and large ways continues to bless the lives of the faithful. We are blessed when we behold how effectively moral witness softens the hearts of those who abuse others. When we experience the positive results of our participation in doing justice, we are blessed with an awareness that we have become co-workers with God for a more just world in which the value of all persons is affirmed.

In, short, when we do justice, we feel authentic!

4. A fourth insight that comes from practicing our faith is that we experience the extravagance of God's grace.

Throughout our society there is the sense that we humans are able to negotiate life's journey to the extent we attune and discipline ourselves to work hard, and that such a work ethic enables us to pull ourselves up by own bootstraps. It's a sense that we are really in control of what happens to us. If we play by the rules of personal responsibility, life will be good for us. Thus, we are led to believe that the quality of our lives is ultimately in our own hands. Some of us may carry this kind of thinking over into our relationship with God, concluding that God will approve and bless us if we hold up our end of the bargain. Moreover, we may even feel that we must prepare ourselves for a relationship with God by cleaning up our act before entering into it in order to have a better chance of making the relationship solid. The bottom line of such an approach seems to be this: Each of us has the power to be successful and it's up to us to make it happen.

This perception seems to miss two very important realities: the inherent weakness of human beings and the depth of God's love. Not only does it assume that we possess the power to lift ourselves up to levels that ensure success and meaning, but it proceeds to imply that God resists responding to us until, by our own efforts, we have done so.

Such a view, I believe, represents a delusion. It places too much emphasis upon human ingenuity and too little emphasis upon God's proactive love. A more realistic assessment of our human limitations and God's grace is made crystal clear in one of Jesus' most popular stories, the Parable of the Prodigal Son (Luke 15:11-32.) The story presents pictures of human weakness in the youngest son who demands his inheritance. Receiving it, he proceeds to waste it in detachment from his family and reckless living. Weakness is also represented in the older son who stays home to assume the responsibilities he has to his father and family. Eventually, however, he manifests a callous self-righteousness that is as damaging as his prodigal brother's recklessness. Thus, the story underscores the insight that human beings have a tendency to mess life up, no matter what moral choices they make.

The father emerges from the dust storm of his sons' mistakes to express love for both. Neither the self-righteousness nor moral recklessness will cause the father to hold back his love. From a distance, he sees his younger son winding his way toward home. What does he do? The father runs to meet him, embracing him in love and forgiveness. Later, when the older son returns from working in the field, he hears the noise of the party thrown for the occasion of the younger son's return; in face of which he cringes with resentment, complaining to his father of his brother's lack of loyalty. In spite of the son's self-righteousness, the father reassures him and encourages his participation in the celebration.

The father's expression of love and acceptance to both his sons conveys to the listener something of about the character of God in relationship to all God's children, namely, that God's love is not a calculated one that turns on and off, depending upon our success or lack thereof. Rather, it is a love so pure that it sees beyond our faults and embraces us because we are deemed precious in God's eye.

I his book, *What's so Amazing about God's Grace,* Philip Yancey describes a conference on world religions where experts from around the world gathered to determine beliefs were unique to Christian faith. They came up with several possibilities such as *Incarnation* and *Resurrection,* and noted that other religions reflected similar doctrines.

Yancey describes the debate continuing for an extended period until C.S. Lewis wandered into the room and asked, "What's the rumpus about? They shared with him their purpose—to determine Christianity's unique contribution among world religions. Lewis responded, "Oh, that's easy. It's grace."

In short, God's grace is God's unconditional forgiveness and acceptance which sprout from a heart completely empty of self-seeking and does not demand anything for itself.

For those of us who have been exposed to tons of conditional love (which Yancey calls "ungrace"), God's unconditional love challenges us with a mystery that defies the logic of conditionality. We may find ourselves spinning in its face until we have experienced its introduction to a transformative new version of reality.

It is significant that, following his experience with the Light as he travelled on the road to Damascus where he aimed to arrest followers of Jesus, Saul spent days contemplating this divine encounter before he was able, with the help of Ananias, to make sense of it (read about it in Acts 9). The experience opened a new world to Saul, who became the Apostle Paul, and we are the beneficiaries of the astounding insight and description of God's grace which the apostle presents in his letters of the New Testament.

Perhaps nothing has been more freeing for me that the experience of God's grace in the form of unconditional love. Not only has it set me free from the paralyzing effects of preoccupation with my own imperfection, but it has empowered me into loving God and committing myself to that relationship without the impediment of guilt. To know that God loves me "warts and all" is to feel such a strong sense of security in that relationship that I can invest in it without fear of failure.

But more must be said. A sure sign that I am in an experience of unconditional love is my extension of that love to those around me through acceptance (particularly of those who are different) and forgiveness of those who have offended me.

In the Great Commandment (Matthew 22:32-40), Jesus reminds us of the integral connection between loving God and loving our neighbor. As a human being, I find it difficult to love like God does, though I continue toward that goal, trusting God's grace to keep prodding and transforming me.

One of my favorite authors, the late Henri Nouwen, defines forgiveness as "love practiced among people who love poorly." In his book, *Return*, he describes this process at work in us:

> *I have often said, 'I forgive you,' but even as I said those words my heart remained angry and resentful. I still wanted to hear apologies and excuses. I still wanted the satisfaction of receiving some praise in return—if only the praise for being so forgiving. But God's forgiveness*

is unconditional; it comes from a heart that does not demand anything for itself, a heart that is completely empty of self-seeking. It is this divine forgiveness that I have to practice in my daily life. It calls me to keep stepping over all my arguments that say forgiveness is unwise, unhealthy and impractical. It challenges me to step over all my needs for gratitude and compliments. Finally, it demands of me that I step over that wounded part of my heart that feels hurt and wronged and that wants to stay in control and put a few conditions between me and the one whom I am asked to forgive.

Loving others as God loves us is demanding. To be successful, one must continue to trust the transforming process the Holy Spirit has established in our hearts which enables us toward that goal. In that process, we become aware that we are not graded on our performance, but accepted in our imperfection while, at the same time, being involved in our development toward perfection.

An experience of God's unconditional love for me, as indicated in The Great Commandment, leads to its inevitable by-product, the practice of love toward others; resulting in the floodgates of meaning being opened through which the cascading waters of purpose and meaning flow into my life.

These four insights to which my faith experience has introduced me have become channels though which God has flooded my life with meaning. Each one addresses a special need most of us have, namely, the need for an attraction strong enough to pull us from our indecisiveness into commitment, the need for a power strong enough to transform our nature, the need for a clear criterion by which to evaluate the level of our spiritual authenticity, and the need for grace that accepts our imperfection.

Because there is a variety in our religious experience, you may highlight other issues that channel meaning into your life. But I suspect that if we all pooled our collective experiences which grow out of our relationship with God, most of what I have identified as *insights* would be common among them. In the case of people from a tradition other than that of the Christian faith, the magnetism drawing them to God would not be so specifically associated with Jesus Christ, but, none the less, the experience of being drawn to God would most likely appear.

While continuing to focus upon our relationship with God as a vein of meaning for our lives, let's shift focus from insights that come to us through that relationship and focus upon how, in our relationship with God, our perceptions of God develop and change.

In a healthy faith-seeking process our perceptions and imagery of God evolve toward a fuller, more satisfying relationship. Most likely, you no longer view or experience God in the same ways you did as a child. As we reflect on the history of our relationship with God, we will conclude that God seems to have grown lot from the time we were children! In my own experience, somewhere along the way, I became dissatisfied with what Bishop John Robinson in his powerful little book, *Honest to God*, calls an "up there/out there," spatial concept of God's dwelling place, i.e., a perception that God is an objective entity that, somewhat like a satellite, orbits the earth from some location in outer space. That concept of God I abandoned long ago. Moreover, I found it necessary to abandon anthropomorphic images of God, including gender images, as I came to realize that God transcends such creature like characteristics. In other words, both in my thinking and experience, God has outgrown such mundane images.

Similarly, the late Bishop John Shelby Spong, discussing the nature of God, challenges what he calls a "theistic definition" of

God "as a being supernatural in power, dwelling outside the world and invading the world periodically to accomplish the divine will."

Such theological reflection as that of Robinson and Spong, has been helpful in my understanding of God as much more than a *being*. Far from invading the world from some vantage point beyond our sky, God, in my experience, is intimately involved in the day-to-day operations of all creation which is most evident on Earth, but also stretches beyond Earth's sky into the wider cosmos.

Far from diminishing my relationship with God, these shifts have strengthened it. For example, on the one hand, they have helped me avoid the trap of cognitive dissonance (the dilemma of ignoring the tension of living with contradiction). On the other hand, the faith which has evolved from my relationship with God has produced a perception that the reality I call God is much larger that I had previously thought. I am convinced that rationalism is limited in its ability fully to access such *ultimate reality*; that faith has a necessary, and complementary, role to play.

As my perception of God has grown, certitude has diminished as a goal of my faith. Most likely, somewhere along the way, you have encountered someone who asked, "Are you sure and certain that you are saved?" Another form may have come as, "Are you certain about your beliefs?" Such need for certitude (which I believe to be a rational category) seems to be popular in some religious settings.

My point is to say that as my perception of God and Godly issues has developed, such rational certainty is neither necessary nor desired. Rather, I have learned the beauty and majesty of *trust* (a faith category) as a response to the benevolent grace of God; especially when confronted with both the mystery of God's magnitude and of life's complexity.

In my experience, faith has moved beyond being defined as a particular system of beliefs or doctrines to a position of leaning into the richness of trusting God's love for me and for all creation. Moreover, the experience has moved me beyond a rule book mentality regarding the conduct of my life and has introduced me to living responsibly by loving immensely, responding to life as a channel of the compassion for God and for creation as exemplified in Jesus as the Christ.

Of course, when, in the process of our evolving perceptions of God and our developing faith, we abandon the presumed certitude of fundamentalism, moralism, dogmatism and the like, there will be times when clouds may diminish our previous certainty. God's will may not be as immediately known. Such times may look and feel like those described by St. John of the Cross when he speaks of the "dark night of the soul" or Mother Theresa's "times of darkness." I suggest that these experiences are more consistent with life's reality than that suggested by the thought that we can live in a bubble of certitude that isolates us from that reality. Moreover, it is my experience that it is the inevitable ambiguity of life that, by its very nature, emphasizes the need for trust which is the root meaning of faith *(pistis)* in the New Testament.

So, in times of such "darkness," with trust in God, I am aware of entering a tunnel with the promise that, at its end, fresh light will come. Therefore, from the tunnel, I continue to pray and to affirm my relationship with God. As a result, I discover that I am not hopelessly lost or inescapably trapped in what Sartre described as a room with no exit.

As we continue our focus upon the rich vein of our relationship with God, I wish now to call attention to two very dangerous traps present along the way of building a relationship with God, traps that have the potential to turn this rich vein from which to extract meaning into an empty well.

As you may already know, our relationship with God requires attention, discernment, discipline and decision. Together, these birth a dynamic relational process that demands careful monitoring, keeping an eye open for those forces that attempt to exacerbate or block the relationship. Two of those traps merit our consideration here: *trivialization* and *marginalization* of God. These two blocking forces constantly cruise our oceans in an effort to torpedo and sink our relationship with the Divine. Because of their threatening pervasiveness, I want to describe them in hope that we will be able to identify and avoid their treacherous grasp.

TRIVIALIZATION: In my thinking, trivialization refers to those attempts to shrink, dwarf or otherwise distort God. Such efforts may grow from our desire to be in control in order to manipulate God for our own ends or to package and sell God to others.

Such attempts to manipulate God are quite prevalent. Human beings want to be in control. That may be our greatest fault. While conversion by its very nature transforms us, enabling us to affirm with reverence the sovereignty of God, such radical transformation is not easy and never instantaneous.

So, the faithful are involved in a process of conversion during which we experience relapses into our "old way" of attempting to be in control. Such relapses may be temporary in which case we recognize what is happening and sharpen our submission to God's transforming Spirit in order to be restored. Such relapses can also become more permanent, particularly if we yield to the delusion that God is simply a divine bellhop ready to meet our every need. In such case, rather than listening to the spiritual clues that we are on the wrong track, we may proceed in the bubble of delusion, all the while rationalizing that because God loves us in such a subservient way, our primary responsibility is to be clear with God about our needs and the ways in which we wish them to be fulfilled. Thus, we attempt to remain in control of a power that can grant all wishes.

There are other ways in which we attempt to trivialize God. Some would argue that churches have attempted to package God in ways that enable them to market God to the masses; thus, attempting to turn God into a slick commodity somewhat like laundry detergent or cough medicine. While that may be an unfair accusation, I can see why some folk in our society may come to such a conclusion.

We who constitute the Church must always be aware that God is not a commodity and certainly not the church's commodity to be sold to the world. Rather, God is the source of the Church's life and that of the world, calling all of us to abundant life which comes on the wings of opening ourselves to the divine Spirit.

Other ways of trivialization are reflected in the ever-present effort among some to limit God to the written word of Scripture or the mind of God to doctrinal or creedal statements. Both Scripture and creed are important witnesses to the nature of God through which the human mind and spirit are inspired and guided. Unfortunately, attempts to equate either to God is to impose upon God limitations that can result in trivialization.

Consider, too, how our language sometimes reflects trivialization. For example, we may hear someone flippantly exclaim, "Oh, my God!" without any apparent reverence for Deity. A closely related example is the pervasiveness of what we in Southern Appalachia use to call "cussin", as expressed in the following ventilation of rage: "By God, I'll get even with you!" or "You are a God damned fool!" Indeed, some folk seem to bend over backward to find new ways to use the sacred name as a way of expressing pent up anger.

These examples are by no means exhaustive descriptions of the numerous ways we attempt to trivialize God. However, they do illustrate how we may, in our own minds, attempt to diminish God. Ultimately this has a devastating effect upon our capacity to be faithful in our relationship to God.

Where does such trivialization come from? Philosophically, I think it is rooted in the soil of theism which defines God as a being, supernatural in power, dwelling outside the world and invading it periodically in order to accomplish the divine will. To my mind, such thinking dwarfs God, reducing God to a size at which we can manage God.

The late Bishop Spong, referenced earlier in this context, calls for an end of theism. In doing so, Spong invites us to perceive God differently:

> *Is it not a possibility worth pursuing that our very self-consciousness might be the means by which our lives could be opened to non-theistic dimensions of our existence, even non-theistic definitions of God? Could not our growing self-consciousness also enable us to relate to that in which our being is grounded, that which is more than who we are and yet a part of who we are? Could we not begin to envision a transcendence that enters our life but also calls us beyond the limits of our humanity, not toward an eternal being but toward the Ground of being including our own, a transcendence that calls us to a new humanity?* 4

I believe there must always be a certain humility present in anyone or anything that speaks of God, lest in our speaking, we trivialize, in one way or another, God's majesty. Such humility leads one to speak of God not with the arrogance of dogmatic certainty, but with understanding that any assertion about God represents, at best, only our finite human perception of God's nature.

Imagine two guys discussing the nature of God, each of whom typically prefaces his statement with "My perception of God is…." Such an approach not only reverences God but in doing so, avoids the kind of dogmatic predisposition represented in the story of two religious persons who realize that they hold deeply different views. So, they strive to convince the other of the validity of their positions. As it becomes clear that the discussion is creating more heat than light, one says to the other, "Brother, we are not making headway with each other. Let's just agree to disagree" to which the other responds, "That's fine with me. You take your point of view and I'll take God's!"

Such unfortunate result comes from a failure to realize that our perceptions of God are just that, perceptions, and must not, therefore, be construed fully to represent absolute truth or ultimate reality.

Theologian Paul Tillich believed that God's full or complete nature defies capture by the human mind. At our best, what we experience are perceptions of God's ultimate grandeur, not the fullness of ultimate reality. Spong reflects this Tillichian insight splendidly when he declares: *To suggest that God and one's own understanding of God are the same is not only to stop growing, it is to die to the quest of truth.*

Failing to understand that principle is to skate on the thin ice of trivialization. In his *Man's Search for Ultimate Meaning*, Victor Frankl calls us to a higher view of God:

> *The concept of religion in its widest possible sense, as it is here espoused, certainly goes far beyond the narrow concepts of God promulgated by many representatives*

of denominational and institutional religion. They often depict, not to say denigrate, God as a being who is primarily concerned with being believed in by the greatest possible number of believers, and along the lines of a specific creed, at that. 'Just believe,' 'we are told,' and 'everything will be okay.' But alas, not only is this order based on a distortion of any sound concept of deity, but even more importantly is doomed to failure. Obviously, there are certain activities that simply cannot be commanded, demanded, or ordered, as it happens, the triad of 'faith, hope, and love' belongs to this class of activities that include an approach with, so to speak, 'command characteristics'."

In his book, *Courage to Be*, Paul Tillich aptly describes our human tendency to make gods of ideas, practices, possessions, and the like, and calls us to cast ourselves upon the "God above the gods" if we are to find optimal meaning in our relationship to Deity. Thus, Tillich reminds us that penultimate gods cannot serve adequately as God. They are only substitutes, and poor ones at that!

Trivialization of God defies the very nature of God as presented in the Biblical tradition. How can we derive positive meaning from relating to a trivialized god, one we can manipulate and one whose destiny we hold in our own hands? That does not work for experiencing a high level of meaning in the relationship we have with God. What does work is to affirm God's greatness and to embrace the relationship that is initiated from the deep and benevolent richness of God.

When we are able to declare "You are God than whom there is nothing greater; to You I offer my praise and my service," we are experiencing a relationship with Ultimate Being. And when we are able to sing, "The One who knows me best loves me most," we feel accepted by that which constitutes the Ultimate on whom our destiny depends and whose essence is love. When we are able to say with the prophet Isaiah the prophet, *"Here I am Lord. Send me,"* we feel embraced by a directing and sustaining power that leads us to experience the deep meaning that lies in the vein of our relationship with God.

Surely, it was a similar experience that led to the writing of such insightful and inspiring passages as this beautiful one:

The Lord is my shepherd, I shall not want. He makes me lie down in green pastures; he leads me beside the still waters, he restores my soul. He leads me in the right paths for his name's sake. Even though I walk through the darkest valley, I fear no evil, for you are with me; your rod and your staff—they comfort me.

*You prepare a table before me in the presence of my enemies, you anoint my head with oil, my cup overflows. Surely, goodness and mercy shall follow me all the days of my life, and I shall dwell in the house of the Lord my whole life long (*Psalm 23—NRSV).

Consider, too, how another psalm reassures us of God's care by picturing God as very near to us in all our circumstances:

O Lord, you have searched me and known me. You know when I sit down and when I rise up, you discern my thoughts from far away. You search out my path and my lying down, and are acquainted with all my ways. Even before a word is on my tongue, O Lord, you know it completely. You hem me in, behind and before and lay your hand upon me. Such knowledge is too wonderful for me; it is so high that I cannot attain it.

Where can I go from your spirit? Or where can I flee from your presence? If I ascend to heaven, you are there; if I make my bed in Sheol, you are there. If I take the wings of the morning and settle at the farthest limits of the sea, even there your hand shall lead me, and your right hand shall hold me fast. If I say, "Surely the darkness shall cover me, and the light around me become night, even the darkness is not dark to you.

For it was you who formed my inward parts, you knit me together in my mother's womb. I praise you, for I am fearfully and wonderfully made. Wonderful are your works that I know very well. My frame was not hidden from you, when I was being made in secret, intricately woven in the depts of the earth. Your eyes beheld my unformed substance. In your book were written all the days that were formed for me, wen none of them as yet existed. How weighty to me are your thoughts, O God! How vast is the sum of them! I try to count them—they are more than the sand, I come to the end—I am still with you (Psalm 139:1-18--NRSV).

A faithful and scholarly Jew, the apostle Paul inherited this tradition of reverence for God. It is not surprising, therefore, that when he visited Athens to wait for Silas and Timothy, he had time to observe the vast array of religious idols and was impressed with the depth of their religious sensibility. In face of it, he declared, *"Athenians, I see how extremely religious you are in every way"* (Acts 17:22--NRSV).

As an apostle of Jesus, he was eager to connect with such spiritual passion. Thus, when invited by some Stoic and Epicurean philosophers to teach them about his own religious convictions, Paul eagerly accepted.

Beginning his address by complimenting their high level of religious inquiry and devotion, the apostle refers to the many objects of their worship as evidence. He calls to mind seeing one altar dedicated "to an unknown god" which leads him to declare:

What therefore you worship as unknown, this I proclaim to you. The God who made the world and everything in it, he who is Lord of heaven and earth, does not live in shrines made by human hands, nor is he served by human hands, as though he needed anything, since he himself gives to all mortals life and breath and all things. From one ancestor he made all nations to inhabit the whole earth, and he allotted the times of their existence and the boundaries of the places where they would live, so that they would search for God and perhaps grope for him and find him —though indeed he is not far from each one of us. For "In him we live and move and have our being," even as some of your own poets have said, "for we too are his offspring." Since we are God's offspring, we ought not to think that the deity is like gold, o silver, or stone, an image formed by the art and imagination of mortals (Acts 17:23b-29—NRSV).

Thus, out of the heart of our biblical heritage we are called to participate in the abundant meaning which comes to us when opening ourselves to the God above the gods, the one who leads us by the still waters and through the darkest valley; the one from whose presence we cannot flee, the one in whom we live and move and have our being.

Clearly, yielding to the ever-present temptation to trivialize God easily distorts and diminishes our relationship with God. When those times come, we need to fine-tune our relationship to the God above the gods, hear the authentic beat of God's drums, and respond with our deepest praise and commitment. It is then we will be able to discover the rich vein of meaning that comes on the wings of relating to God.

MARGINALIZATION: A second trap we must avoid, one that is equally poised to diminish the quality of our relationship with God, is reflected in our tendency to see life as divided into two segments, the sacred and the secular, concluding that we can detach God from the mainstream (often thought to be the secular) and confine God to the narrow strip we call sacred.

Such a flawed sacred/secular division produces the assumption that we can live in the arena of the secular without much, if any, reference to faith which is thought to be limited to the sacred dimension. In this scenario, we may think of ourselves as living, for the most part, in the secular realm only to enter the sacred for spiritual assurance or refreshment.

I have always been intrigued by the way in which members of the Italian Mafia have been characterized in popular cinematic productions. Their lavish lifestyles are supported by criminal activity that exploits the general population—drugs, money laundering, prostitution, and the like. Turf consciousness leads them, at the drop of a hat, to murder any adversarial competitors. Interestingly, they are frequently pictured as deeply involved in the life of the Church, as reflected by the high esteem they exhibit toward baptisms and confirmations while displaying their bare-chested crosses. Frequently, I come away from such exhibitions feeling that I have witnessed the art of attempting to marginalize God through a neat bifurcation of life into clearly distinct sacred and secular sectors.

But one need not join the mafia in order to practice such compartmentalization of life. I suggest that there are folk at every level of the socio-economic spectrum who have similarly divided life into two watertight sectors, attempting to separate the sacred from the whole of life.

I shall never forget an experience in Nashville, Tennessee, in the early 1960's, when hundreds of like-minded folks committed to social justice, joined in a march to the mayor's office. Those were the days when segregation kept thousands of citizens, especially African Americans, from access to many of the city's public amenities. Our aim was to express to the city leaders our strong desire to open Nashville's public swimming pools to all citizens regardless of their ethnicity. So here we were, a gaggle of students, teachers, blue and white-collar workers, and interfaith clergy on the move. Since there were many clergy dressed in their distinctive. collars, the religious orientation of the participants was obvious.

As we made our way between Vanderbilt University and the downtown area, we were greeted by crowds of people gathered along the street to protest our demonstration. I was struck by the anger reflected in so many red-faced scowls, shaking fists, cursing, etc. One man exclaimed, "Why don't you people stay in your pulpits and churches? Why are you out here in the streets causing trouble?" It was obvious that this person knew little or nothing about the relationship between our faith and its call for social justice and the public square. To me, it seemed that as far as he was concerned, we were attempting, inappropriately, to bring spiritual matters outside places of worship into the mainstream of public life. I suspected that, to him, there was a clear-cut division in life between the sacred and the secular and that any attempt to bridge the two was to be vigorously resisted.

Beyond these examples, there are other ways we attempt to marginalize God. Sometimes, without much thought and reflection, we fall into such a preoccupation with everyday life and its demands for food on the table, sustaining a career, paying the mortgage, educating the children, and preparing a nest egg for retirement, that we simply crowd God out of our awareness.

Consider what we do with our children. Because we love them, we want them to have a good education, good medical care, friends, social skills, etc. In the process of focusing upon those issues, we fail to nurture their capacity for dealing with failure, practicing forgiveness, caring for others, being in awe of mystery, and the like. As a result, when life comes at them hard, they frequently have difficulty adjusting.

For years, I was so invested in my career that I missed some opportunity to share time, experience, and wisdom with my children. Oh, I loved them then, as now, but at the time I was so preoccupied with ensuring their material future that I came up short in nurturing other important dimensions of their needs. Have you ever heard yourself exclaiming, "If I had it all to do over again, I would….!" Of course.

Perhaps, even now, you find yourself becoming so preoccupied that God is getting crowded out of your life. I know that feeling well, and am constantly protecting myself from such grievous error.

I have a good friend who, in his writings, has shared his preoccupation with finding self-worth through a feverish pursuit of higher education. Earning his college degree left him feeling bereft. Completion of his first graduate degree did not solve the problem. After earning his PhD, his self-esteem continued to register low. He still had not found a strong sense of self-worth. It was then that he began to reflect upon his dilemma. One evening, while staying in a hotel during his visit to a university to deliver a lecture series, he began to focus his attention upon God. All night long, he struggled and, in the wee hours of the morning God broke through all the scar tissues of his life and he was able to hear God declare, "John, you are precious to me. I love you. You have tremendous worth, already. You don't have to earn it."

My friend agrees that the experience brought transformation into his life and that God whom he had held at bay for so long through preoccupation, was now front and center. What had seemed to be an insatiable search for self-worth was finally being satisfied through an experience of God's accepting love.

From this chapter of his life John has proceeded to teach in some of our most prestigious universities, to serve as pastor of some of our finest congregations and to have an outstanding writing career.

As we continue to talk of attempting to marginalize God, I feel compelled to share this: There are those who believe in God, but whose concept locates God so far beyond our everyday world that there is little (if any) possibility of a God/human relationship. It is a philosophical marginalization of the Deity which emerged out of the Enlightenment. Such deism gets expressed as, "I believe in God, but not a personal one."

Through the years I have encountered these folk and found them to be quite interesting. I find that, usually, they have had such difficulty with more popular theistic concepts of God that they have felt compelled to opt for an alternative view. One person expressed the dilemma this way: "I don't feel at home with a view of a supernatural God who encourages followers to be in a state of passive dependence upon his care; yet I can't imagine there is no God. I could never be an atheist."

Have you encountered these folks? Perhaps you, as I, appreciate their honesty. I do get the feeling, however, that such a philosophical marginalization renders a god with which a relationship is either non-existent or extremely limited.

When Tillich steers us away from conceptualizing God as a personal being, he is not moving toward a view that would perceive God as an impersonal force—as a mechanical law of nature that keeps the universe running smoothly. Rather, he is beckoning us to experience God's transpersonal nature, a nature deeper and unlimited as though God is an ocean of personhood, the Ground of

Being—in whom we live and move and have our being.

Now let us note that, while Scripture acknowledges a distinction between creature and Creator, there is also the affirmation that the Creator seeks a relationship with that which is made; yet that relationship is portrayed not as a "good buddy" one between two equals. Instead, it is one in which the creature, while experiencing the Creator's indescribable love and acceptance, is able to trust and affirm God's awesomeness while living with the unanswered questions that follow in the wake of recognizing the majesty of God.

In the Bible, a story from the book of Exodus (33:17-33) provides an example of this quality of relationship with God in an experience of Moses who expresses his strong desire to see God face to face. At this point in the story Moses has experienced God only in such natural phenomena as a cloud, thunder or lightening. Now God's response to his interest in a face-to-face encounter, is to prohibit it, indicating that such an experience would result in the death of Moses or, for that matter, any human being. Finally, Moses is allowed to behold "the hind parts" of God as God passes the area where Moses is hidden in the cleft of a rock.

Throughout Scripture, God is portrayed as having a concern for all creation and a desire to establish a relationship with all of it; particularly with human beings. For example, the prophets portray God as seeking people in order to establish that relationship. Then, when one comes to the New Testament, God—the invisible, majestic, beyond the limits of verbal or symbolic description— comes to creation in the life of Jesus as the Christ. Consider, for example, this passage from the Letter to the Hebrews:

Long ago God spoke to our ancestors in many and various ways by the prophets, but in these last days he has spoken to us by a

Son, whom he appointed heir of all things, through whom he also created the worlds. He is the reflection of God's glory and the exact imprint of God's very being, and he sustains all things by his powerful word" (1:2-3a—NRSV).

All this is to say that while God cannot be contained in our human vocabulary which by its nature is culturally created and culturally shaped, we must not conclude that God must, therefore, be banished to a region beyond human experience or perceived only in impersonal, mechanistic images.

Bishop Spong, in a chapter entitled "Beyond Theism but Not Beyond God," asserts, "If 'otherness' is a part of who or what God is, then God must be a presence that, while it can be experienced, can never be defined." 7 Hence, to my mind, Spong avoids the mistake of deism (the marginalization of God by effectively affirming the distinctiveness of God *vis a vis* created things, while, at the same time, emphasizing that we can experience a relationship with God.

Let me now draw to a close in chapter one by declaring that my relationship with God, initiated and established through God's love and grace, is the primary relationship of my life from which I derive my value as one of God's beloved, along with my purpose of glorifying God in all things in my stewardship of life, my stability as one who is secure in God's acceptance and approval, my blessing as one who cherishes all God's fulfillment, including everything from daily sustenance to the blessing of my human relationships, and my destiny to become everything God created me to be both in this life and the life to come. In short, my relationship with God is an unlimited vein I am endeavoring to mine that my life will be filled with meaning and purpose.

In this chapter I have shared with you much of my personal

context through which faith was born and nurtured. From there I shifted to share some of the life-giving insights growing out of my faith experience. I have also called to attention two very dangerous traps to be avoided in our journey with God, traps that can dwarf the quality of that journey.

With an eye on the central role of our relationship with God in finding meaning for our lives, I want to conclude with an observation made by St. Augustine: "O God, our hearts are restless until they find their rest in thee."

CHAPTER TWO

Our relationship with Others

When St. Augustine prayed, "O Lord, our hearts are restless until they find their rest in thee," he seemed to sense, as do we, that experiencing a positive relationship with God is foundational in our search for meaning. Is this meant to minimize or to exclude our relationship with one another as a source of meaning?

As we participate in a community of faith, we soon discover at its center a commitment to loving God, and at the same time, loving one's fellow human beings so aptly symbolized in the vertical and horizontal shafts of the cross of Jesus. There, the vertical piece emphasizes that we are committed to that which is transcendent, namely God, who is simultaneously present, while the horizontal shaft emphasizes our commitment to one another. From that angle of viewing the whole cross, this important symbol underscores the importance and the inextricability, of loving God and loving one another. Those two relationships are symbiotic, indeed.

The theological foundation holding these two relationships together is made clear in Jesus' Great Commandment, given in Matthew 22:37-39—NRSV):

'You shall love the Lord your God with all your heart, and with all your soul, and with all your mind.' This is the greatest and the first commandment. And a second is like it: 'You shall love your neighbor as yourself.'

You may be aware that this is Jesus' response to a question put to him by a fellow who was both a religious scholar and a lawyer: *"Teacher, which commandment in the law is the greatest"* (verse 16)?

The exchange illustrates Jesus' remarkable capacity for distilling voluminous religious teachings to their essence—loving God and loving others. Thus, he concludes the conversation with this astonishing observation: *"On these two commandments hang all the law and the prophets"* (verse 40)

From the context of his discussion with the religious scholar, I understand Jesus to be saying two things: (1) that our relationship with God is the primary pillar supporting our discovery of meaning, but that our relationship with one another, while being secondary, is an extremely important corollary, and (2) that the essence of our journey of faith—what it's all about—is loving God and one another, not in getting lost in a maze of religious red tape.

With this incident between Jesus and the scholar, then, let us explore the following issues: Jesus' commitment to the integral connection he sees between our love for God and our affirmation of one another, what loving others looks like, the inadequacy of selective loving, love's vision of a new kind of community, the temptation to find meaning in isolation from others, and the implication of the love commandment for forgiving one another.

Loving God and Others as One: Let's examine the basis for Jesus' welding together of these two components. One of his goals seems to be that of simplifying what had become complex. In his first century context there were literally hundreds of commandments, obedience to which was considered necessary for a right relationship with God and others. Not so with Jesus who seems concerned that such religious legalism had seriously eroded the inspiration and power of a great faith tradition by placing too much emphasis upon religious laws and performing religious duties.

Legalism, whether in the first century or our own, seems always to create a rule-book mentality which limits the power of faith to flood its adherents with meaning.

Close observation of Jesus suggests that he is thinking of two things in his exchange with the religious scholar— simplification of what had become a complex religious system and a more effective way of thinking about our relationship with God.

His simplification technique is to distill hundreds of the accumulated commandments into two extremely sensible and relevant obligations for one who wishes to live responsibly before God. In the process, Jesus is offering an alternative way of interpreting what it means to be faithful, namely, opening ourselves to God's loving acceptance in such a way that we are able to adopt that lifestyle. Thus, his insight reflects a conviction that our status before God is not determined by how well we perform in obedience to rules—as though God withholds love until our performances reaches the level of divine approval—but by opening ourselves to God's love up front. This opening up, transforms and enables us to become channels through which that same kind of love flows both toward God and others.

When I contemplate that, I conclude that Jesus' simplifying work, along with its ability to correct our course, must continuously be offered in each generation given the tendency of religious folk to drift into a legalistic mindset that returns us to a wilderness of religious complexity.

Jesus' ability to cut through the jungle of theological and ethical red tape is very impressive. This grasp of God's intent seems to be an important source of his inspiration and power for such bold effectiveness. He was an astute student of Scripture, knowing the creation stories along with their reflection of Eden's paradise, as well as its loss. As a faithful Jew, he knew the Jewish law; how it was initially given and how it had developed and expanded through the ages to his present time. As a prophet himself, Jesus knew the long line of prophets and their hearts as well. From his call of duty and empowerment by God's Spirit, he actualized his authority over the law and the prophets (see Mark 9:2-8 with its story of "The Transfiguration"). Now, in this passage and in his role as a great teacher, Jesus reaches profound but clearly understandable conclusions about the importance of loving both God and one another in the journey of faith.

His commitment to loving God was deeply rooted in how he understood and experienced God's distinctive nature As Creator, God is in a unique category of reality from all things created. God is God. All else is creation. God is ultimate. All else is penultimate. As the Ground of Being, God is Pure Being. All else is only a form of Being, although it participates in and reflects God's Being. Therefore, for Jesus, God is to be revered and loved above all and with all.

Far from being despised because it is less than God, creation is to be affirmed and valued. Created things are not evil, but inherently good. Jesus was familiar with how the creation stories (Genesis 1 and 2) convey God's pleasure with each step of creation when, as each is completed, the narrative declares, *"God was pleased with what he saw"* (Genesis 1:9-10—Today's English Version).

Thus, Judeo-Christian faith holds that materiality and physicality, characteristics of all created things, are not evil, but good. God is perceived to derive significant delight in their presence. Following the distortion of creation's perfect harmony, God is seen as caring so deeply that God intensifies his process of healing. So, as Adam and Eve, burdened by guilt, hide in the forest, God does not ignore nor reject but, with a loving heart, comes looking for them.

Jesus reflects this high view of creation when, in The Great Commandment, he gives such prominence to the call not only to love God but to love others as well, fully aware that Adam and Eve, as we, belong to the category of creation.

While Jesus' teaching here is fresh, it is not new. That which is fresh is not an emphasis upon our need to love God and one another. Aspects of this divine expectation can be found throughout the Old Testament. In fact, Jesus' reference to loving God and loving others is a quote from Deuteronomy 6:5 and Leviticus 19:18. What is distinctive about his teaching is the way in which he weaves the two together into one garment and presents them as the highest expression of what it means to be a person of faith. Thus, both he and his disciples seem very clear that love for God and for one another cannot be separated. Listen for the deep conviction detectable in this Johannine declaration:

For we cannot love God, whom we have not seen if we do not love others, whom we have seen. The command that Christ has given us is this: whoever loves God must love others also (John 4:19b-21—Today's English Version).

What Loving Others Looks Like: Let's zoom in the character of this love for others. What behavior toward others does it create and energize? How wide is its scope? How does produce meaning for us?

One image of loving others is that of becoming a person for others. In observing Jesus' ministry, one is soon able to detect that he was a man for others. When I observe the lives of his serious and inspiring followers, whether it is St. Francis of Assisi, Albert Sweitzer, Martin Luther King, Jr., Billy Graham, or scores of less famous disciples—relatives, friends, teachers, pastors, physicians, and numerous other saintly sages, I experience inspiration in their examples of being a person for others.

Every such person seems to recognize in others a dignity which must be honored and a precious dimension that must be valued. Such recognition calls forth our willingness to make a commitment to the well-being of others, even when it demands a stretch into uncomfortable zones. Such lovers seem not to allow others to be perceived as adversaries on the journey or competitors in the pursuit of well-being, but as neighbors to be valued and souls to be nurtured.

A touching example of stretching to love those who see themselves as our adversaries is found in Dr. King's "A Christmas Sermon on Peace," delivered December 24, 1967 at the height of the civil right rights movement:

> To our most bitter opponents we say, "We shall match your capacity to inflict suffering by our capacity to endure suffering. We shall meet your physical force with soul force. Do to us what you will, and we shall continue to love you. We cannot in all good conscience obey your unjust laws, because non-cooperation with evil is as much a moral obligation as cooperation with good. Throw us in jail, and we shall still love you. Send your hooded perpetrators of violence into our communities at the midnight hour and beat us and leave us half dead, and we shall still love you. But be ye assured that we will wear you down by our capacity to suffer. One day we shall so appeal to your heart and conscience that we shall win you in the process, and our victory will be a double victory. (HHTP://Portland. indymedia.org/en/2003/12/276406.shtml) 1

Loving others does not mean becoming intimate with every person one meets. One of my favorite writers is Thomas Merton who until his untimely death in 1968 was a Trappist monk at the Gethsemane monastery in Kentucky. His many books include *Thoughts in Solitude, New Seeds of Contemplation, Zen and the Birds of Appetite, No Man Is an Island,* and his best-selling autobiography, *The Seven Story Mountain.* In *No Man Is an Island,* Merton reminds the reader that it is unrealistic to form a limitless number of intimate friendships. He believed that most of us have only a hand full of such, along with a greater number of friendships at various other levels. But we are enabled by God's loving Spirit to hold all others, even those we don't know well, to be of value. In his own words:

> *We can be, in some sense, friends of all men (sic) because there is no man on earth with whom we do not have something in common. But it would be false to treat too many men as intimate friends. It is not possible to be intimate with more than a very few...."* 1

But, like Jesus, Merton emphasizes the importance of affirming all others with love. Consider, for example his chapter entitled "Love Can Be Kept Only by Giving It Away" in which he shares the following descriptive statements about loving others:

A happiness that is sought for ourselves alone can never be found: for a happiness that is diminished by being shared is not big enough to make us happy....

Love not only prefers the good of another to my own, but it does not even compare the two. It has only one good: that of the beloved, which is, at the same time, my own....

To love another is to will what is really good for him....

Charity, (by which I take Merton to mean expressed love for another) *is neither weak nor blind. It is essentially prudent, just, temperate, and strong. Unless all the other virtues blend together in charity, our love is not genuine....*

It is clear, then, that to love others well we must first love truth.... (The truth of which Merton speaks here is, in contrast to abstract speculation, the mortal truth that) *...loving our brothers is the concrete destiny and sanctity that are willed for them by the love of God....*

Charity makes me seek for more than the satisfaction of my own desires, even though they be aimed at another's good. It must also make me an instrument of God's Providence in their lives....

In order to love others with perfect charity I must be true to them, to myself, and to God....

A selfish love seldom respects the rights of the beloved to be an autonomous person....

Charity must teach us that friendship is a holy thing, and that it is neither charitable nor holy not to base our friendship on falsehood....

When all has been said, the truth remains that our destiny is to love one another as Christ loved us....

> *Perfect charity gives supreme praise to the liberty of God. It recognizes His power to give Himself to those who love Him purely without violating the purity of their love. More than that: selfless charity, by receiving from God the gift of Himself, becomes able, by that fact alone to love with perfect purity...."*[2]

From these excerpts from Merton's writing, it is clear that, while we cannot be intimate with all those around us, we can love them, and that love is not some diluted tipping of the hat to their existence but a firm concern for their welfare that elicits from us sensitivity and affirmative acts of caring. Our love for others is not simply having a good feeling for them, to endorse all their styles of living, to love them because it makes us feel good, or to love them in order to take advantage of them. Loving others is always proactive, self-giving and unconditional, reflecting both the mind and behavior of Jesus. Moreover, it is love that far, from diminishing appropriate self-esteem, calls for a valuing of the self, strong enough to serve effectively as the criterion for the quality of our love for others.

Selective Love Falls Short of True Love's Vision: As I reflect upon Jesus' ministry and the character of the community of faith that sprang up around it, so soundly nourished by the apostles and extended into or own time, I realize that the love ethic contained in The Great Commandment continuously critiques and corrects our imperfect practice of it. One example of that imperfection is our tendency to select particular persons to love while ignoring those who are less attractive to us. From the beginning, followers of Jesus, like most human beings, have struggled with racism, sexism, ageism, etc., all of which are examples of such selectivity.

Ugly marks of our failure to love others more completely are reflected in those times, early in the civil rights movement in the United States when men guarded the doors of churches to make sure persons of color, particularly African Americans, did not gain entry. While only a few churches practiced such exclusion, there was a strong scent of prejudice that permeated the air of some communities and some of us who were around in those days could smell it on ourselves, as well as others. While we have come a long way from those days with both our public and private institutions, there continue to be pockets of racist people among us.

These days, especially for church folk, I sense a shift of focus from racial prejudice to a bias rooted in our long-standing homophobia. This prejudice is reflected in a variety of ways, including the suspicion among some including church people, that homosexual persons are not normal and, therefore, inferior. This assumption has been a root cause of so many of the discriminating practices in our society, including our reluctance to accept the validity of same-gender loving relationships.

We are aware that there are religious folks who are on the forefront of the struggle for liberation from sexual prejudice -- similar to the brave and faithful folks who led the civil rights movement. Yet, there are many in religious communities who resist such liberating efforts. Visible in the resistance are persons whose perception of what it means to be faithful leads them to the conclusion that to be a homosexual person disqualifies one from leadership positions in church life. On the broader scale, their perceptions lead them to believe that, since marriage between same gender persons is forbidden, spousal-like civil and legal privileges should not be granted to them.

It is not surprising, therefore, that most (but not all) major religious denominations are experiencing considerable struggle as they seek to discern God's direction through the maze of issues with which sexual prejudice and discrimination confront us.

While these issues reflect an ancient struggle, there seem to be fresh signs, both in religious institutions and in the wider culture, that we are attempting to be more affirming of others and especially those who are different. For people of faith what seems fresh is the struggle over the legitimacy of same-gender relationships rooted and sustained in mutual loving commitment. Among people of faith there is a growing sense that the long-standing discrimination against such same gender relationships is not consistent with the core values of Judeo-Christian faith. Important questions are being raised about how to practice love and acceptance toward and with those who challenge some of our most deeply seated sexual precepts ingrained over time. Many persons of faith are feeling led by God's Spirit to be more open to the Spirit and less bound by tradition in engaging these issues. In turn, these fresh developments raise a very significant related question: How do we respond to our acquaintances who continue to resist these fresh approaches and, therefore, seem content with the status quo? 3 It seems to me that the same spirit leading us to be more accepting and inclusive needs to shape our response to those who have not yet embraced acceptance. Otherwise, we may find ourselves in that untenable position shared by the guy who exclaims, "I am tolerant of all people except those who are intolerant!" The growing spirit of acceptance is challenging us to reevaluate our rejection of those who resist it.

In other words, the persuasive spirit of acceptance is challenging us to reevaluate the responses to others offered by tradition's discriminatory stance. Our faith's call to love others unconditionally as God loves us, along with its implications for relating to those whom tradition has not held in high esteem, is proving to be a strong force. For example, increasing numbers of the faithful feel that we are being called to trust love's sensitivity to all others; not just to the targets of discrimination but also to those who are the discriminators. We are becoming more aware that, in the forward moving power of acceptance, there is the ever-present danger of reverse discrimination.

I detect growing desire among the faithful to work for a deeper sense of community among all people, giving special attention to the points at which sexual preference results in continuing fragmentation and division. The practice of acceptance and community are gaining momentum and opening fresh avenues of healthy relationship among a huge variety of people and lifestyles. I believe the promise of reconciliation and unity for the future is bright. The brighter it gets the deeper the quality of our life together becomes.

Love Directs Us Toward Others: While there are people who seek the meaning of life by moving in a direction which takes us away from others, the Great Commandment, with its focus upon loving God and one another, draws us toward them. How can we love God by moving away from God? How can we love others when we move to isolate or insulate ourselves from them?

This leads me to distinguish between a common need for withdrawal to rest and relax, on the one hand, and withdrawal to separate, isolate, and escape, on the other. We may hear someone exclaim, "I need a vacation!" or "I wish I could go to some distant island away from the noise and den of people where I may be able to find myself!"

Who among us has not found it helpful to withdraw into places of solitude better to tune into God? And have we not all felt a need to withdraw from society's pressure cooker in order to get back in touch with ourselves? But, in my experience, these moves are not meant to be permanent as though I might better find God in isolation. Rather, they are experienced as strategic steps aimed at restoring myself for a positive return to fellowship with others, joining with them in finding meaning in the ups and downs of everyday life.

Do you remember how Jesus is pictured as removing himself

periodically from the larger group in order to become more centered for his mission? In one such case we are told *"...he dismissed the crowd. And after he had taken leave of them, he went into the hills to pray"* (Mark 6:45-46—NRSV).

The benefits of finding such an oasis for renewal are obvious to those of us who have escaped from our routines in order to find renewal for reentry. Such a strategy seems wise, indeed.

On the other hand, what concerns me are those who feel they must abandon the human community in order to find meaning. I remember hearing a sermon by United Methodist Bishop Gerald Kennedy in which he told of a parishioner who felt the only way she could find God was to succeed in getting away and staying away from people during which, in a moment of sheer exasperation, she exclaimed, "Bishop, I love God but I can't stand people!"

In telling the story, the bishop was highlighting the contradiction of searching for a purer relationship with God by divorcing oneself from involvement with humanity.

Some history may be instructive here. At the very beginning of what would become the monastic movement, a second century Egyptian by the name of Anthony, who is thought to be the founder of monasticism, seemed to be motivated by the need to get away from other human beings in order to find God. Over time, however, adjustments to the rationale for monasticism were made that affirmed the integral connection between a monk's love for God and for precious humanity which God so deeply values. Monks began to see one of their purposes to be that of prayerful support for those on the front lines of faithful work in the world. As a result, the world beyond the monastery has become an important focus for those who dwell in prayer and contemplation behind the monastery's walls.

Consider too that Transcendentalism a la Henry David Thoreau of Walden Pond fame has sometimes been mistakenly interpreted as running away from community into isolation in order to experience the meaning of nature. Rather, Thoreau seemed to be interested in offering a corrective alternative to becoming lost in the masses and their tendency to drift away from the beauty of nature with its opportunities for renewal of mind, body and spirit.

I sense in Jesus' commandment to love God and one another a theological response to a human tendency toward bifurcated living in which we choose one to the exclusion of the other. In The Great Commandment, I hear Jesus calling us to experience the gifts for combining our love for God and others. It is not an either/or situation, but a both/and. As a result, the more I love God, the more precious others become to me. On the other hand, the more I practice compassionate service with and to others, and the celebration of authentic community with them, the more precious God becomes.

Love's Vision of a New Kind of Community: Those struggles with barriers that separate human beings from one another are not new. Wherever one enters the stream of human history, they are there. The New Testament reveals their pronounced presence in the first century. Indeed, the issue was one of the factors moving Jesus to emphasize the need for loving others as we love ourselves. He envisioned his followers as people who genuinely interacted with one another in love. To bring that vision into reality he had to be intentional in confronting the very real shortcomings of their thinking and behavior. For example, among his apostles were many of the usual issues that cause conflict—ethnic and class prejudice, selfish ambition, desire for instant gratification, self-righteousness, etc. Jesus constantly confronted such community-destroying issues by teaching his beloved a better way to find the abundant life of meaning that God wills for all people.

St. Paul, Jesus' self- proclaimed apostle to the Gentiles, had a special knack for picking up on various aspects of Jesus' teaching, developing and applying them to the situation in which early disciples found themselves. A good illustration is the way in which he developed the concept of the Church as a new kind of community called to reflect Jesus' vision of equality and justice. Take, for example, the passage in his Letter to the Galatians in which he declares:

As many of you as were baptized into Christ have clothed yourselves with Christ. There is no longer Jew or Christian, there is no longer slave or free, there is no longer male and female; for all are one in Christ Jesus... (Galatians 3:27-29a—NRSV).

The apostle's view is that God is birthing a new kind of community—to be distinguished from society at large—in which God enables the faithful to live without the barriers so common in the larger society. When the Galatian letter was written, around 50 A.D., the dominant barriers dividing people were ethnic (Jews/Gentiles), economic (slave/free, poor/wealthy, common/ privileged), and gender (male/female). Those barriers spawned others, perpetuating centuries old divisions which created astounding injustices and sucked dignity and meaning from the lives of people all across society.

Being a strong apostle of Jesus, St. Paul believed that this new Jesus-envisioned society without barriers would grow to challenging barriers wherever they were found. It is clear, both from his writings and our own experience, that the ideal has not yet been achieved; that there continue to be pockets of resistance to living without them, even within the faith community. What has been achieved in the faith community and the broader culture is a compelling vision whose magnetism continues to draw us toward its reality. Look at our national and world history. Behold the march of justice and equality that continues to invade the strongholds of those who are determined to defend the barriers.

Persons of various Christian denominations and Faiths believe so strongly in the unifying vision that they are working diligently to practice the love that gives its coming reality momentum, all the while daring to believe that at some point life without barriers will be achieved. For Christians, this belief is renewed every time we pray, *"...Thy kingdom come, thy will be done, on earth as it is in heaven...."* and every time our behavior reflects a spirit of inclusion rather than exclusion.

The Implication of Love's Vision for the Issue of Forgiveness: Unforgiveness is an entangling jungle in which so many of us spend a large portion of our lives. As we have journeyed alongside other people, we have encountered persons filled with a high level of anger and resentment from which they strike out; sometimes offending us deeply.

In his book, *What's So Amazing about Grace*, Philip Yancey shares some very interesting examples of what he calls unforgiveness. He tells of a woman who refuses to visit her sick father who is dying from a diseased liver caused by extended alcohol abuse. Although he has been sober for years and has turned his life around, she continues to be so traumatized by his earlier abuse that she refuses to let him off the hook.

Yancey also tells of a mother who has vowed never to have anything else to do with her son because he chose in early adolescence to adopt a drug infested life of criminality. Though he has made overtures toward her, she has rejected every one and maintained a consistent posture of unforgiveness.

There are times when scenes of unforgiveness are not so dramatic. I remember hearing a story of an old fellow who spent the last decade of his life sleeping down the hall from his wife. Thirty years earlier a rift had occurred over whether had had shown enough concern for their five-year-old daughter's illness. Neither of them will take the first step toward reconciliation. He lies awake each night waiting for her to approach him while, down the hall she is waiting for his appearance. They tragically remain in their two different worlds because neither will forgive.

Can you remember a time when you were entangled in the web of unforgiveness? Are you now resisting forgiveness from someone who has offended you? Some of us have memories of such entanglements long since resolved. Others have not found a way of escape, and continue to feel caught in a spirit of unforgiveness that ferments within them, producing noxious odors of anger, resentment, and restlessness. Some who have not escaped unforgiveness may find themselves suddenly awakened from sleep remembering an offense and its effects as it plays in living color upon their mental screens. Their days may be marked with an ill temper, a sharp impatience, and a cloud of preoccupation.

I am convinced that such an experience so profoundly affects the human psyche that, in some cases, we may come to a point of marshalling our resentment with which to feed what has become a crusade which, in turn, has become our purpose for living. Though the experience produces a hellish emotional chaos, we embrace and feed on its poison in such a way that our spiritual vitality is drained. No wonder there are so many people with such short fuses!

In face of this plea to abandon unforgiveness, someone may say, "But, that's so naïve. Forgiveness does not take seriously the depth of offense!" Such response seems so terribly delusional to any who know the destructive power of unforgiveness to the complex circuitry of our being.

In *What's So Amazing about Grace*, Yancey tells of his participation in a conference of ten Jews, ten Christians, and ten Muslims led by the author and the psychiatrist M. Scott Peck. The hope was that a sense of community or the beginnings of reconciliation may emerge. Yancey reports that neither did. Instead, fist fights almost broke out as the Jews talked about all things done to them by the Christians, and Muslims about the horrible things done to them by Jews, while Christians tried to talk about their own problems which paled in contrast to the Holocaust and the plight of Palestinian refugees. Yancey reports:

> *At one point an articulate Jewish woman, who had been active in prior attempts at reconciliation with Arabs, turned to the Christians and said, "I believe we Jews have a lot to learn from you Christians about forgiveness. I see no other way around some of the logjams. And yet it seems so unfair to forgive injustice. I am caught between forgiveness and justice."* 4

This person reflects the ambivalence of many who glimpse at a way of escape from the entangling jungle through forgiveness; yet remain skeptical, given the serious injustice of some offenses.

Such dynamics make forgiveness difficult. How does one get over the hurdle of injustice while running toward the goal of forgiveness? Perhaps the answer lies in a direction articulated by St. Paul:

If someone has done you wrong, do not repay him with a wrong.... Do everything possible on your part to live in peace with everybody. Never take revenge, my friends, but instead let God's anger do it. For the scripture says, 'I will take revenge, I will pay back, says the Lord' (Romans 12:17-19--TEV).

In the case of how to respond to one who has deeply offended us, I sense that the apostle is asking us to entrust to God the role of justice maker. It's a decision to leave the scales that balance justice and mercy in God's hands when it's too complex for us to handle; then return to continue working toward forgiveness.

But what has the power to move against the grain of injustice and its pain all the way to forgiveness? It's the power that moved Nelson Mandela to pursue peace rather than justice when he had been elevated to power in South Africa. Pope John Paul 11 reflected it when he descended into the depts of Rome's Rebibba prison to visit Mehmet Ali Agea, a would-be assassin who nearly succeeded in killing him. There, Pope John Paul spoke these words, "I forgive you."

It's the power of love that, when complemented with the faithful relinquishment of vengeance to God, blooms into forgiveness.

That act of loving another enough to forgive is an inescapable dimension of The Great Commandment. That act of love gains remarkable power from its antecedent in the commandment, namely, loving God with all our being. The commandment not only weds loving God with loving others, it also joins God's forgiveness to our responsibility to forgive others.

In God's forgiveness we have a model for our own, a model which communicates its power, enabling us to forgive. Consider, for example, the Parable of the Unforgiving Servant (Matthew 18:23-35) in which a servant is forgiven a debt of several million dollars. Immediately, the servant proceeds to look for a fellow servant who owes him only a few dollars. Finding him, he demands payment, but the debtor cannot and asks for mercy. Rather than to extend mercy, he has his fellow servant thrown into jail. When the king learns of the injustice, he orders his servant's arrest, exclaiming to him: *"You worthless slave! I forgave the whole amount you owed me just because you asked me to. You should have had mercy on your fellow servant, just as I had mercy on you."* (vss. 32-34). Then the king has him thrown into jail to be punished. Jesus underscores the profound importance of the parable's teaching when he concludes: *"That is how my Father in heaven will treat every one of you unless you forgive your brother from your heart"* (vs. 39). Thus, the parable challenges us to consider the magnitude of forgiveness.

St. Paul has that issue under his scope as he writes of God's forgiveness as foundational:

For when we were still helpless, Christ died for the wicked at the time God chose. It is a difficult thing for someone to die for a righteous person. It may even be that someone might dare die for a good person. But God has shown us how much he loves us—it was while we were still sinners, that Christ died for us! By his blood we are now put right with God; how much more, then, will we be saved by him from God's anger! We were God's enemies, but he made us friends through the death of his Son. Now that we are God's friends, how much more will we be saved by Christ's life! But this is not all; we rejoice because of what God has done through our Lord Jesus Christ, who has now made us God's friends (Romans 5:6-11—TEV).

In Jesus' parable it is clear that the servant had the right to collect the few dollars his fellow servant owed him. Throwing him into jail was his legal right. While not disputing the legality of the situation, Jesus wants his followers to see their own loss in light of God's forgiveness of a much larger debt; thus, making the point that only the experience of being forgiven provides the power and motivation for us to forgive in return. In other words, only in the experience of God's magnificently redeeming love are we able to extend the same to others. It is completely illogical that we could experience such forgiving love without passing it on. It makes perfect sense to extend what has bathed us in its magnificent splendor to others, no matter what they have done.

A miracle of grace occurs when, recognizing the love of God, we open ourselves fully to receive it. That recognition delivers us to return love to God and to extend it to others as unconditionally as we received it from God. With practice, such receiving and giving of love becomes a way of life. Somewhere along the way we begin to understand the profound wisdom of Dostoevsky who said, *"To love a person means to see him as God intended him to be."* 5

When I was a youngster, my grandmother kept me busy with chores. Occasionally, one of those chores was to go into the cellar and inventory the stock of food she had canned and sealed in Mason jars. More specifically, my assignment was to discover those that had spoiled because of losing their seal. I was to take those and empty their foul-smelling contents onto the ground prepared to receive them; then return the jars to her to be washed. I remember the excitement of getting rid of the bad stuff and seeing the jar, freshly washed, restored to its crystal-like beauty.

That distant memory becomes a parable for an experience of forgiving. It's like pouring out all the stuff that is poisoning our system, thereby restoring the beauty and meaning of our lives.

There are few things more precious than walking through the blessed gateway of forgiveness, returning to that person who has been estranged and effortlessly embracing them while realizing that the one who was once considered an adversary is now a friend. At that point I know that loving others as God loves me is to experience the power of faith that moves huge mountains of unforgiveness.

Like our relationship with God which we explored in Chapter 1, our relationship with others constitutes a mine filled with abundant veins of meaning. For most of my life I have been digging here to identify and appreciate that meaning. It's a process that I continue to engage.

As a result, I continue to enter each day with hope and excitement, clear that my purpose is to cultivate those relationships. In doing that I am aware that my life is not simply the product of my parents' biological union, but expands into a purposeful journey that finds its meaning, grounded in my relationship with God, which includes my experience of community with other human beings and, as we will see in the chapter that follows, community with wider nature.

The rich veins of meaning that lie both in my relationship with God and others seems inexhaustible. The longer I live and the more I work the mine of these life-giving relationships, the more blessed and precious life becomes, for I am constantly being nurtured with an abundance of purpose and meaning.

Having considered our relationship with God and with others, let us now move to a consideration of our relationship with nature.

CHAPTER THREE

Our Relationship with Nature

It may seem that when we shift from considering our relationship with God and with others, to that with nature, we have moved into a distinctly different territory altogether. Perhaps in some ways we have, but in more important ways we have not, for there is an integral connection among the three categories.

From the perspective of Biblical faith everything in the world comes from God's intentional design. In that design, not only do all things have purpose, they are objects of God's redeeming love as well. In that way all things are connected both to God and to one another. However, in the Biblical perspective, the Creator is always perceived to be distinct from creation, in order to make clear that God is not a created entity. This distinction is extremely important in each of the three major religions with roots in the Abrahamic tradition—Judaism, Christianity, and Islam. Each cautions the faithful against mistaking any created thing for God. At their heart, these three agree with the spirit of the second commandment of the decalogue:

You shall not make for yourselves an idol, whether in the form of anything that is in heaven above, or that is on the earth beneath, or that is in the water under the earth. You shall not bow down to them or worship them" (Exodus 20:4-5a—NRSV).

Thus, the Creator's distinction from all creation is carefully guarded.

To see God and creation as two distinct categories of reality is not to suggest, however, that God is aloof from creation. From the beginning of the biblical story (Genesis 1 and 2), all things created originate in God's intentional choice and are sustained by God's considerable care. The two creation stories dramatically present the Creator as approving each aspect of creation and moving to establish a relationship with it. Moreover, after human beings are created, God calls them to establish relationships among themselves and with other species of the natural world.

It is to our relationship with the other species within nature that we now turn. In perceiving nature as a distinctive category with which to relate, care must be taken not to distinguish too sharply between human beings, on the one hand, and nature on the other, for there is a special connection between the two. Maintaining an awareness of this important connection will enable us better to extract the optimal meaning nature has to offer us.

I bring two key assumptions to this consideration: (1) human beings are a part of nature, and (2) many other of nature's species have the capacity of relating to us. For example, some non-human forms of nature reflect the capacity for feeling or experience while others possess an inner subjectivity similar to consciousness.

I invite you to look more closely at the implications of these two assumptions:

Human Beings Are a Part of Nature: Is there a fundamental divide between humans and nature? To be sure here are distinctions among the various species, but is there a degree of difference that merits the placing of human beings apart as though we constitute a unique category in creation?

There is evidence that, at times, human culture has answered in the affirmative. One of the consequences of such a response is the emergence of a view that human beings are so exceedingly superior to the remainder of nature that we transcend nature.

While that perception may have multiple roots, one is a popular interpretation that the Bible's account of creation emphasizes the uniqueness of human beings because we are bearers of God's image. Some have jumped from that platform to the conclusion that humans are under a divine mandate to control nature for our own ends.

Let's take a closer look at the issue. The book of Genesis (chapters 1 and 2) gives us two accounts of God's creative acts. In the first account, human beings are brought into being only after everything else has been created. They are given special responsibility with respect to the remainder of God's creation:

So, God created humankind in his image, in the image of God he created them; male and female he created them. God blessed them, and God said to them, "Be fruitful and multiply and fill the earth and subdue it, and have dominion over the fish of the sea and over the birds of the air and over every living thing that moves upon the earth. See, I have given you every plant yielding seed that is upon the face of the earth, and every tree with seed in its fruit; you shall have them for food. And to every beast on the earth, and to every bird of the air, and to everything that creeps on the earth, everything that has the breath of life, I gave given every green plant for food." And it was so (1:17-30—NRSV).

The second account offers new information. For example, God

creates man out of the dust of the earth, places him in the Garden of Eden; then creates woman:

In the day that the Lord God made the earth and the heavens, when no plant of the field was yet in the earth and no herb of the field had yet sprung up—for the Lord God had not caused it to rain upon the earth, and there was no one to till the ground, but a stream would rise from the earth, and water the whole face of the ground—then the Lord God formed man from the dust of the ground, and breathed into his nostrils the breath of life, and the man became a living being. And the Lord God planted a garden in Eden, in the east; and there he put the man whom he had formed…. Then the Lord God said, "It is not good that man should be alone, I will make him a helper as his partner." So out of the ground the Lord God formed every animal of the field and every bird of the air, and brought them to the man to see what he would call them; and whatever the man called every living creature, that was its name…. So, the Lord God caused a deep sleep to fall upon the man, and he slept; then he took one of his ribs and closed up its place with flesh. And the rib that the Lord God had taken from the man he made into a woman and brought her to the man (2:4b-8,18-19,21-22—NRSV).

I have placed these two stories of creation before you not only to reacquaint you with their content, but to point out that they share both similarities and dissimilarities. For example, in both accounts God is affirmed as the Creator, with human beings sharing a special responsibility for the remainder of all created things. Only in the second account do we get a specific description of man and woman being created and placed in the garden of Eden to dwell.

These are beautiful stories from two different sources. Their purpose is to cast light upon God as the source of all things that came into being and upon the interrelationships all these things enjoy. Therefore, these stories stand tall in our sacred history, not so much for their scientific accuracy—for they come from a pre-scientific era—but for the rich theology they convey.

However, what I and others consider to be misinterpretations of the stories' intent have caused problems over the centuries, particularly at the point of how we human beings are to relate to other manifestations of nature. For example, some have interpreted the first of the two accounts as a precedent for the superiority of human beings over the remainder of God's creation, citing the following instruction from God to the man and woman: *"Be fruitful and multiply, and fill the earth and subdue it, and have dominion over the fish of the sea and over the birds of the air and over every living thing that moves upon the earth"* (1:28). From the raising of human beings to a point of superiority, it is a small step toward what has proven to be a disastrous conclusion that humans, therefore, are destined to manipulate and even to exploit nature.

That interpretation has opened a Pandora's box of consequences. The presumption that humans are above or superior to nature has resulted in some who view themselves as nature's masters to the extent that they proceed to utilize her—even to the point of abuse—to satisfy human needs. That kind of thinking has spawned such misfortune as uncontrolled strip mining, overfishing of our seas, and reckless deforestation.

Interpreting the creation accounts in such a way that human beings are given the right to set ourselves above the natural world to utilize it for our own selfish ambitions is increasingly incredulous.

Thankfully, in recent years we are witnessing the emergence of a powerful alternative perspective reflected in a growing consensus that we humans are not above nature, but are an integral part of nature.

In his book, *The Nature Principle*, Robert Louv articulates this alternative perspective eloquently and persuasively. He describes the increasing aversion of any human versus nature dichotomy: "Inevitably (these days), the context is shifting from humans and nature, to humans in nature, and humans as nature." 1

Theologians have been effective critics of the notion that the Biblical accounts of creation distinguish human beings from the rest of nature in such a way that suggests a precedent for humans to become her exploitative masters. Consider this article published in "Interpretation" (October 2011) and quoted in *The Christian Century:*

> *Christians typically think of humans as stewards of creation, says Theodore Hichert, and Old Testament professor. That view, based on the Genesis 1 account of creation, needs to be counterbalanced by the Genesis 2 account of creation. In the latter account humans aren't portrayed as stewards over creation, but as an integral part of and servants of nature. In the second account, humans aren't created in the image of God as the crowning achievement of creation; rather, they are formed out of the fertile earth just like other forms of life. This view of creation emphasizes human interrelatedness with nature and the need to serve it rather than use it to serve human needs." 2*

I appreciate Professor Hitchert's insight. It underscores the connection of human beings to other species of nature and presents creation as a beautiful garment resulting from the interweaving of all species into a whole. He does this without diminishing the important role of the creator and the creator's love for all created things. HItchert's thinking makes the stories less vulnerable to division represented in the view of those who tear humans from the bosom of nature and set them apart as manipulators.

We must be careful not to pit the two accounts of creation against one another. While they are distinct accounts of creation faith, they are woven together in the first two chapters of Genesis in such a way that they complement each other. The reader does not have to choose one over the other. While the first account does describe humans as living under a mandate to care for all creation, it would be a mistake to interpret the arrangement as a license for abusive manipulation. When we consider the entire creation account (both stories) we are led to see the emergence of a stewardship concept which suggests that humans are designed for partnership with the rest of nature in which various species experience mutual responsibility to care for and benefit from the gifts offered to one another. Some may bring more gifts to the table than others, but all bring gifts to be offered for the good of the whole.

Professor Hitchert's insight that we humans are a part of nature and servants to nature—as opposed to being above nature and destined to manipulate or exploit her—is profoundly significant. It beckons us to view and experience all elements of nature as pleasing to God. It also invites us, with respect and care, to serve the various expressions of nature in such a way that all creation is ultimately enhanced.

In that context, stewardship becomes not only a human responsibility, but the responsibility of all elements of nature toward each other. In this view there is a stewardship to be exercised by humans, one to be assumed by undomesticated animals, and even one that belongs to the weather. With each element serving the other, all nature is able to move forward together, assuming mutual responsibility for the well-being of the whole.

In theological terms, all of nature is able to join God in a move toward the eschatological vision of *"a new heaven and a new earth"* (Revelation 21:1) which symbolizes redemption, the God-intended maturity and harmony of all created things. Theologian Jurgen Moltmann holds our move toward this eschatological vision to be very significant. He believes that God's creative work —always ongoing—is designed to bring all of creation to perfection. It is not surprising that one of his most popular books is titled, *A Theology of Hope*. In another of his works, *The Future of Creation*, Moltmann speaks of the completion and perfection of creation, promised by God, envisioned and worked toward by those who share such purposeful faith. The achievement of that goal is described with powerful eschatological imagery which, for people of faith, becomes a dynamic source of energy motivating us to be stewards of nature, behaving toward her responsibly and in very practical ways. In that process, we actively participate in bringing to fulfillment the prayer of Jesus that God's kingdom will come and God's will done *"on earth as it is in heaven."*

In chapter 8 of The Future of Creation, Moltmann describes creation (nature) as an open system whose eschatological redemption is enhanced when we humans move to see ourselves in symbiotic relationship with her:

> *Justice is the form of authentic interdependence between people, and between society and the environment. It comes into being in the symbioses between different systems of life, and is the basis for common survival. Its presupposition is the recognition and subjectivity of the other life systems.... We human persons need each other within communities. We—human communities—need each other with the community of mankind. We—the creation—need God, our Creator and Redeemer. Mankind faces the urgent task of devising social mechanisms and political structures that*

encourage genuine interdependence, in order to replace the mechanisms and structures that sustain domination and subservience. 3

The bottom line is that human beings join other manifestations of nature in sharing mutual responsibilities for the good of the whole. This becomes a fertile field of experience and understanding in which we are able to affirm the interdependence (complementarity) of all species, realizing the precious dignity and promise of each, along with our responsibility to serve one another.

Various Manifestations of Nature Reflect the Power to Relate to One Another:

The thought of relating to other natural species is not new but, now, I am sensing a fresh dynamic at play, that of forming those relationships as partners in the adventure of shared life, a situation vastly different than one derived from the assumption that humans are superior to and masters of other species of creation.

Richard Louv believes that the development of what he calls "an ecological unconscious" is feeding this fresh dynamic:

> *The idea of an "ecological unconscious" now hovers above the crossroads of science, philosophy, and theology— the notion that all of nature is connected in ways we do not fully understand. In his 1841 essay, "The Over Soul," Ralph Waldo Emerson wrote of "the great nature in which we rest, as themselves earth lies in the soft arms of the atmosphere, that Unity, that Over-soul, within which every man's particular being is contained and made one with all other; that common heart." 4*

This is a description of interdependency and commonality among nature's species which resists the adversarial imagery of power invasions from vantage points of superiority that attempt to control, exploit, and abuse.

In such a context, relational experience among natural species flourishes. We are able to sense in other species an inner subjectivity, i.e., the possession of the qualities of consciousness, or experience and feeling, or a combination of all.

While we recognize the valid distinction between the plant and animal kingdoms, research is showing the astounding capacity of the various species for relating across the borders of those kingdoms. This is not to suggest that plants and humans can interrelate just as humans to with one another, but it makes room for the concept of species within the plant kingdom do respond positively to human care and vice versa.

Louv affirms the existence of these plant/human relationships and notes that we are often unaware of them. Referencing Michael Pollan's book, *The Botany of Desire*, he points out that we human beings should balance our sense of self-importance with the fact that we are a "plant dependent species." From there, he shares an insight from Charles A. Lewis', *Green Nature/Human*, in which Lewis declares, "*the chlorophyll molecules of green plants bear an intriguing similarity to hemoglobin, the prime constituent of mammalian blood.*" 5

My late mother-in-law loved orchids. Dedicating an entire room of her Santa Fe, New Mexico home to them, she called them "my children." In that humidity-controlled environment she raised them with tender love and care. Frequently, I would hear her say, "I've got to go talk to my children. They respond so well when I talk to them and show them how much I love them." She had the reputation of having the most beautiful orchids in town!

Then, consider our relationship with other mammals. Once, it seemed that non-human mammalian species were largely devoid of subjectivity and that only humans could think and reason, but research is showing quite the opposite.

For at least a decade the general population has become aware that research involving dolphins has confirmed their ability to relate other species, including humans. This, along with other important research, is yielding growing evidence that the perceived gap between humans and other animals is narrowing.

In June, 2012, Associated press science writer, Seth Borenstein's report headlined, "Evidence Piles Up Showing Primates Act Similarly to Us" appeared in my city's *Sarasota Herald Tribune* announcing that animal research is pointing out that we humans seem less special than we have earlier imagined:

> *The evidence that animals are more intelligent and more social than we thought seems to grow each year, especially when it comes to primates. It's an increasingly hot scientific field with the number of ape and monkey cognition studies doubling in recent years, often with better technology and neuroscience paving the way to unusual discoveries. This month, scientists mapping the DNA of the bonobo ape found that, like the chimp, bonobos are only 1.3 percent different from humans.* 6

Referencing the research of Duke University scientist, Brian Hare, Mr. Borenstein proceeds to cite examples showing how ape and chimp behavior reflects their ability to exercise a combination of reason and memory. Amusingly, he writes:

> *At the National Zoo in Washington, humans who try to match recall skills with an orangutan's are humbled. Zoo associate director Don Moore says, "I've got a PhD, for God's sake, you would think I could out think an orangutan and I can't!"* 7

What happens to the capacity to relate when we move from

the organic realm into what modern science has traditionally considered to be the material world of dead, inanimate matter? In his work, *Universal Feeling*, a PhD dissertation prepared for the faculty of Emory University, John H. Buchannan addresses this question. Buchannan examines two of the 20th century's most distinctive perspectives, those of Stanislav Grof's transpersonal psychology and Alfred North Whitehead's speculative philosophy. With a goal of emphasizing that life is designed with purpose, adventure and hope, a contrasting perspective to *"the modern world's denial of soul or experience as a primary operative factor in the universe,"* 8

Buchannan interfaces these two figures to show that both Grof and Whitehead object to the traditional characterization of inanimate matter as dead, and, thereby, to affirm the implication that there is "universal feeling." Buchannan proceeds to describe how Grof and Whitehead, together, envision all nature as alive and subjective, possessing the power for relational experience.

In our ordinary state of consciousness, we often appreciate inanimate nature, but imagine only ourselves to be subjectively involved with inanimate entities perceived only as objects of our response to their appeal. Buchannan's research into Grof and Whitehead convinces him that the potential in this relationship can be developed into something more significant and life-giving as we move beyond an ordinary state of consciousness to a higher state. This higher state of consciousness, according to Buchannan, sensitizes us to the relational capacity of inanimate matter as it transports us to a more contemplative and reflective state of mind to which Grof refers as a "holotropic" mode of consciousness.

While there are differences in Grof's and Whitehead's perceptions of how we can experience the various species of nature and how they experience us, they agree that the interfacing among the species occurs, underscoring their conviction that even inanimate nature cannot be accurately described as dead.

Grof expresses his viewpoint in the following:

> *Experienced extension of consciousness in the holotropic mode is not limited to the world of biology; it can include macroscopic and microscopic phenomena of inorganic nature. Subjects have repeatedly reported that they had experientially identified with water in rivers and oceans, with various forms of fire, with the earth and mountains, or with forces unleashed in natural catastrophes, such as electric storms, earthquakes, tornadoes, and volcanic eruptions. Equally common is identification with specific materials—diamond and other precious stones, quartz, crystal, amber, granite, iron, steel, quicksilver, silver, or gold. These experiences can extend into the micro world and involve the dynamic structure of molecules and atoms ... even electromagnetic forces and subatomic particles.... It seems that every process in the universe that one can observe objectively in the ordinary state of consciousness also has a subjective experiential counterpart in the holotropic mode. 9*

Now, turning to Whitehead's perspective, Buchannan writes:

> *He (Whitehead) attributes subjectivity and creativity to all actualized entities, and envisions a persuasive conscious Being, i.e., God. But for him, the "inner subjectivity" of matter is conceptualized as being essentially experiential or feeling in nature, rather than as a form of consciousness with its implications of reflexivity and self-knowledge. 10*

As I understand it, Grof's point is not that consciousness and creative intelligence are products of inanimate matter, but that inanimate matter plays a crucial role in the entire fabric of existence because of its effect upon us when we approach it in an elevated state of consciousness.

If my understanding of Grof is correct, I can report that I have experienced this higher state of awareness by means of contemplation on various occasions. One occurred in the chapel of Kentucky's Gethsemane monastery. I was there on a spiritual retreat which included some conversation with Thomas Merton whose writings in the area of contemplation have enabled thousands to access the deeper dimensions of life and faith.

One evening, as I sat alone in the chapel contemplating the beauty of God's love, the flame of the alar candle took on a peculiar hue and movement. It appeared to become more than a mere burning candle and seemed to be transformed into a fountain of inspiration as it transmitted waves of grace-filled warmth. The ordinary flame became to me a living thing, full of meaning. Initially, with my natural vision, I saw just the burning candle, but its beauty and the response it aroused within me magnified and blossomed as I journeyed beyond my ordinary state of consciousness into a higher holotropic one. That experience, like an inexhaustible source, continues to feed and expand my consciousness beyond the ordinary into a vast and inspirational dimension that sharpens my sensitivity to wider reality and stimulates my anticipation for what lies ahead.

Indeed, our ordinary state of consciousness that feeds upon our sensory experience can be rich, but when one moves beyond sensory perception into a non-ordinary or holotropic state, one's perceptions and experiences are deeply enhanced. In my experience, faith as a trusting openness to life's deeper mysteries (and adventures) is the avenue through which I am able to journey into a holotropic state of consciousness and to experience the capacity to access what is often hidden in an ordinary state. (Just now, as I write, there comes to mind Jesus' promise to lead us to the peak of abundant life. For me, a dimension of that abundancy is the capacity to move beyond ordinary states of consciousness to the higher one Grof calls *holotropic*.

Tap into your own memory to see if you have had similar experiences in which you have discovered the personality of inanimate entities. It could have been a star-lit night, a waterfall, a mountain, a rising or setting sun. I suspect you are in touch with such an experience, and that calling it forward into the present serves as a blessing.

Buchannan's careful analysis and description of the interface between Grof's transpersonal psychology and Whitehead's organic philosophy has increased my sensitivity to a relationship between ourselves and all other natural realities, both those considered animate and inanimate. The conclusions reached by the spiritual and intellectual integrity of those sensitive souls have helped me stretch beyond what is considered ordinary and stimulated me to an intentional focus upon the potential for relationships which, in earlier years, I was not sensitive enough to discern. The experience has enhanced my own quest for meaning.

I hope that you, too, will become increasingly sensitized to nature and motivated to explore the relational possibilities she provides. To do so is to mine a vein of meaning that has the capacity to enrich our lives considerably. Our relationship with nature deepens our appreciation for the wonder of all creation. The experience of its many gifts continues to inspire volumes of music, drama, and literature, giving us a growing sense that, as a part of nature, we move with all our natural counterparts toward a destiny of promise.

As the 18th century English poet Alexander Pope contemplated the story of Jesus' turning water to wine, he remarked, "The conscious waters saw their Master and blushed." For me, the poetic power of that description has come to represent nature's capacity to relate to us in inspirationally cogent ways that communicate an invitation to sharpen our sensitivity to the majesty that surrounds us, to embrace its dimensions, and to join the adventurous journey of hope, expectation, and meaning.

And so, I submit to you the elaboration of the two assumptions with which I approach this chapter focused upon our relationship with nature: (1) That we human beings are an integral part of nature, and (2) that the various manifestations of nature reflect the power to relate. For me, these assumptions have opened the doors to a magnificent oasis of meaning. Hopefully, they will do the same for you.

My Experience with Nature: I was born in a place and time that provided me with opportunity to be in touch with nature. Southern Appalachia is full of mountains, streams, and various species to which I had ample access. Village life in the 1940's and the 1950's amplified nature's invitation to participate in her many gifts. Before the advent of television, computers, and cell phones, those days pulled us into the "outdoors" to mingle with livestock, gardens, caves, grapevine swings, swimming, fire-fly catching, medicinal root digging, barefooting, fishing, hiking, and the like.

Seasons had their distinctive opportunities for our interrelationship with nature. Spring was filed with the aroma of bud and bloom. Summer offered swimming holes and leafy forests. Autumn painted the hills and mountains with breathtaking colors and provided fluffy mattresses of pine needles, along with vast carpets of leaves in which to scurry and scuffle. Winter brought deep layers of snow extending to frozen creeks and ponds that became expansive rinks for skating.

In that setting, nature touched me in such a pervasive way that its various manifestations became a friend with whom my buddies and I intermingled throughout the day and night as we closed out our evenings on our backs gazing up at the stars.

When I awoke each morning, I could see the sun rising over Beech Mountain and proceed to release the flow of its light down the slope of Elk Valley toward me. Along the way, like a flood, the light engulfed the sloping heights of Double Knobs before rushing directly into my bedroom and awaking my senses to the dancing waters of nearby Curtis Creek while the orchestral sounds of birds celebrated the birth of a new day. What a marvelous foundation for building a life in touch with nature!

But such foundational experiences would not have been as influential without a mentor who massaged my sensitivity to that environment. That mentor was my dad who encouraged my brother and me to "get out there and enjoy all the good things with which we are surrounded," and then often joined us in the venture.

My brother and I continue to talk about those trips into the wilderness with Dad. Vivid in my memory is the first time we traveled to the top of Beech Mountain which stood prominently at the east end of Elk Valley. No matter what we were doing during the day, we often cast our eyes upon its pinnacle which beamed a smile upon us. There was an enduring quality to the mountain. The only discernible changes were in its color during the seasons, ranging from the rich green of springtime to the brilliant colors of autumn and the snowy white caps of winter.

One summer day, dad declared, "Boys, this coming weekend we're going to hike to the top of Beech Mountain!" Our delight was fervent. When the day arrived, we drove the old Pontiac to a point near which we began our hiking ascent. From there, through the foothills, we walked a trail leading to a remote place where the Lee family lived. Soon, we could hear the sounds of children playing when Dad remarked, "These children have never been off this mountain. They rarely see anyone from the outside I don't know how they will react to us when we break out of our forest shelter into the open where they can see us." Then, it happened: as soon as we stepped into open view, they scurried in every direction to hide from us. As we passed, I could see little heads peeking from behind rocks and trees to observe us as we continued our journey.

Soon thereafter, we came to the base of the mountain and, without the benefit of trail or marker, Dad led us in a circuitous but certain direction as though guided by an internal compass implanted by his own childhood experiences with his father. For the most part, we wove our way through an abundance of Poplar, Oak, Maple and Hickory trees which had grown to immensity through beds of rocks and boulders covered with beautiful moss that clung to their base like protective garments of soft, rich green. Occasionally, we glimpsed the scampering of squirrels and ambling racoons, along with an assortment of lizards, all of which seemed to acknowledge our presence with only the slightest curiosity.

Eventually, we came to a small opening in the forest canopy from which we could see the "Hogback," a protrusion of granite, located about halfway up the mountain. Clearly visible from our village, we often admired it from afar. Now, we were just a few hundred yards below it. From this perspective, it seemed to tower directly over us like some gigantic creature watching our every move. Soon, I became aware that I was looking straight up at it and it was as though I could feel its cold breath upon me, triggering a slight chill of anxiety. Sensing his sons' apprehension, Dad ushered us right up to Hogback's base where he reached out and touched it, inviting us to do the same. From that time on, that which we had perceived from a distance to be a grotesque hernia on the Beech's belly became a friendly and respected protrusion of ancient granite destined to inspire and guide any hiker to continue toward the pinnacle of the mountain.

As we continued our ascent, we felt the thinner air and the increasing demand to breathe deeper. Soon, we noticed a marked change in the species and size of the trees. Hickories and Oaks gave way to Beeches, a much smaller member of the native tree families. They seemed less grandiose but more friendly. Forming a less dense forest and being not much taller than us adventurers, their canopy was so porous that we could see clearly the mountain's pinnacle at a distance. There, among the Beeches, the boulders gave way to smoother terrain. Much to our surprise, beautiful grass spread like a well-laid carpet throughout the area inviting us to run, jump, tumble and roll.

To this area we would return for the night, but, presently, we pressed on toward the pinnacle whose granite fist thrust from the mountain to form what to my imagination, was a salute to the heavens. Standing as close to the summit as we could get, we were able to see the Blue Ridge Mountain range snaking its way northward. Looking at a wider screen than I had ever witnessed, I stood in awe of the panorama that unfolded before us. Reflecting the wisdom sensitive fathers possess, Dad kept silent, along with my brother and me, enabling us all to feel the inspiration of nature's grandeur. It was a silence deliciously seasoned only by the screeching of a distant hawk as it sailed high above us upon an ocean of air. Soon, Dad spoke, "Boys, behold the beauty with which the Good Master has surrounded us. Don't ever ignore it; always respect it and be thankful." Although that statement impressed and inspired me in the moment I heard it, little did I know how those words would continue to influence my attitude, even to this day, affecting my experience, not only of the wilderness, but also of

God and my fellow human beings.

The ecstasy of that pinnacle experience was followed by our return to the earlier described grassy spot. We explored the area, examining various kinds of plants, bugs, and worms. Also, we noted that with the exception of the large hawk, the birds seemed to be much smaller than those in the valley. With that, we began our preparation for the evening and the night.

After clearing an area and erecting a makeshift shelter we built a fire and warmed the food which Mom had prepared for us. Soon we found ourselves wrapped in some of Dad's wonderful stories. There, with our dad and enveloped in family love on top of the mountain we viewed daily from the valley, we shared impressions of the day. As we basked in the warm security of that setting, our day drew to a close as we watched the brilliant sparks from the fire fly upward, beyond the dwarfed trees, to disappear silently in the night sky.

My brother and I have never forgotten this and other wilderness experiences we enjoyed through the years. Presently, as I describe these bygone scenes, they seem to leap across the decades into the present and continue to nurture my spirit.

These childhood experiences prepared me with a sensitivity toward the natural world that continues. Now, in the latter stages of my journey, I often reflect on how I took time to be in touch with nature in every stage. I've introduced my children and grandchildren to it, and followed Dad's counsel always to appreciate and never take for granted the beauty with which the Good Master has surrounded us. Indeed, nature continues to be a vein from which I extract a strong sense of meaning.

I identify so closely with an observation Richard Louv makes early in his *The Nature Principle:*

As a species, we are most animated when our days and nights on Earth are touched by the natural world. We can find immeasurable joy in the birth of a child, a great work of art, or falling in love. But all of life is rooted in nature, and separation from that wider world desensitizes and diminishes our bodies and spirits. Reconnecting to nature, nearby and far, opens new doors to health, creativity, and wonder. It is never too late. 11

Now, as we draw near to this chapter's end, please join me in some reflective time. Louv has long been convinced that many of us moderns live with a "nature deficit disorder." What we need, he insists, is a strong dose of nature ("Vitamin N," he calls it), —more green in schools, and more access to nature in communities. He is convinced that we have an innately emotional affiliation (biophilia) to other living organisms, including the natural landscape.

Focusing more specifically upon how a positive relationship with nature brings healing, Louv references research at Deakin University in Melbourne, Australia, concluding on the basis of their anecdotal, theoretical, and empirical research, the following:

Exposure to natural environments, such as parks, enhances the ability to cope and recover from stress and recover from illness and injury.

Established methods of nature-based therapy (including wilderness, horticultural, and animal-assisted therapy) have success healing patients who previously had not responded to treatment for some emotional or physical ailments.

People had a more positive outlook on life and higher life satisfaction when in proximity to nature, particularly in urban areas. 12

In a review of Louv's work appearing in a 2012 summer edition of *Newsweek*, Andrew Weil writes:

The term "nature deficit disorder" was invented by Richard Louv…to point out a deep truth as participants of our evolutionary heritage, human beings—both children and adults—have a profound need for time in wild, outdoor spaces,, and we suffer when we don't get it…I see much evidence that nature deprivation is a major driver of many negative psychological trends, including the modern epidemic of depression"

Recognizing the remarkable gifts that a healthy relationship with nature has brought to my life, I continue to devote significant portions of each day being in touch with her and letting her touch me. In our travels, my wife Beverly and I identify targets in which involvement with nature is available, whether in the great Northwest of the United States, the Nile Valley of Egypt, the Jordan gorge with its river's flow into the Dead Sea, the Nabatean civilization of Petra, or the hills of Galilee in Israel.

At the end of each day, about an hour before darkness falls upon our community in Sarasota, our five-pound Yorkshire Terrier, Moose, and I head out for our evening hike. Just a few minutes into our journey we leave the streets and houses to enter a zone full of lakes, lush fields of green grass and trees. Moving into the open areas where the grass is a bit higher, Moose changes his gait from a fast walk to that of leaping to avoid bulldozing through the grass and to have a better view of the surroundings. The speed of my gait is also increased, not only to keep us with Moose, but to respond to the adrenalin of excitement which comes with being in the midst of such natural beauty.

Along the way, we encounter majestic Sandhill Cranes travelling in pairs. During the birthing and nurturing season, they are alert to protecting their chicks who follow closely, waiting for a delicious morsel freshly dug from the earth by their long beaks to be passed from mom or dad to their open throats. On such an encounter, as I stand watching their ritual, my heart is warmed with the amazing ways in which nature instills in this species such nurturing and protective instincts.

On our way, Moose and I behold two young otters playing in the lake. With the shimmering of their wet backs and the fluidity of their rolling movements, they remind me of the toy slinkies which were so popular during my childhood. Observing them, I am impressed by how much the sounds of their frolicking are much like those of children at play.

Coming to a view of an island that sits in the middle of the lake, Moose and I notice that many of the bird species have begun to roost in its bushes. Scores of white birds have already taken their places while others, like airplanes, glide in a circle preparing to land. The island seems to be in motion with the transformation of its usual green into a beautiful white, giving it the appearance of a large basket of white magnolias afloat.

On another evening as Moose and I round a corner between two lakes, there, lying on the trail about 20 yards in front of us is a dark, stubby, and muscular snake which I immediately identify as a Water Moccasin, a highly venomous species. Though it is lying still, it seems to sense our presence and is now in traveling mode, not a coiled, restful one. It appears to have just crawled from a marsh filled with bushes, heading toward the nearby lake. Moose who is highly sensitive to anything appearing to be a snake (including strings or long tree branches) remains as still as I until I take him in my arms to carry him around the snake, giving it a wide birth, until we are safely beyond it. A few steps later, looking back, I notice that Mr. Water Moccasin has left the scene.

Everywhere, near the lake shore and under the clear water, I notice bowl-like indentations in the sand carved out by the fanning fins of Tilapia for the laying of their eggs. As Moose and I walk along the shore, we observe a parent Tilapia floating atop its nest. Nurtured and protected, the eggs will soon be transformed into playful babies darting through the water with remarkable speed and energy.

Returning home, Moose rushes to his water bowl for a sumptuous drink accompanied with loud and vigorous lapping that defies his size and demeanor. By the time he finishes, I'm relaxing in my chair with a cold drink. Here he comes, jumps onto the hassock to hunker down against one of my legs, taking care, through a series of moves, to get as close to me as he can. Reflecting on the richness of our journey into nature, I conclude that one of the finest, most meaningful experiences with nature is that with the remarkable and loving little creature I call Moose.

My brother and I frequently speak of our experiences with nature, shared since we were children. Recently, he said to me. "Our lives have been so enriched by our wonderful experiences of God's beautiful creation. I can't imagine life without them." I concurred. Moments later, we were on a beautiful golf course listening to the sounds of an osprey shouting at us from a nearby tree.

CHAPTER FOUR

Some Key Dynamics of Our Relationships

This book is based on the proposition that the meaning of life is found in our relationships and, particularly, our relationship with God, others, and nature. To this point our focus has been upon the life-giving character offered by each. Now, I'd like to take an additional step. Recognizing that these categories of relationships—each having its own distinctive character—are not designed to stand alone, let us explore how they interrelate.

Imagine what your life would be like with God as your only focus. Ask the same question of the other relational categories. When I do that I get a picture of significant limitations. Our biblical faith, sensitive to such misfortune, calls us to value God supremely but, along with that, to value one another, and the vast sea of creation (nature) that surrounds us.

All of this suggests that there is such a connection between each category that, if we attempt to limit ourselves to any one of them to the exclusion of the others, we not only weaken its life-giving power but we become unbalanced in our approach to life. In other words, there is such a built- in connection among the three that, to pluck one from its symbiotic harmony with the others would result in consequences not unlike attempting to steal a heart or liver from the human body. In short, these three relational categories are designed to work together to produce abundant meaning, capable of empowering a useful and purpose filled life.

I recognize he truth of this principle when I reflect upon my own journey. For example, as a child, the loving relationships I enjoyed with my parents helped me to understand the nurturing influence of God's love. As I matured to experience the unmerited love of God, I learned something about the richness of my parents' love for me.

This rich process ushered me beyond my immediate family to explore my relationship with other people, ways to be open to those with whom I felt acceptance, but also how to respond to those with whom I felt tension or a potential for it.

Then, there is the world of nature. While I didn't think so much about the beginning of this relationship I cannot remember when I didn't love nature's beauty, and the opportunities she offered for a richer life experience. From the outset, my rich relationship with her seemed to be rooted in a recognition that she was designed by the loving hand of God. Through the years I have been enhanced by the presence of family and friends who have participated in awe of her magnificence. Whether it was being thrilled by swinging on a wild grapevine, swimming in a river, hiking a trail, beholding a colorful caterpillar, or admiring deer families relaxing under a shade tree.

The point is that there is such an interconnection among all three relational categories that an experience of one necessarily opens us to an experience of the others in such a way that, together, they offer abundant meaning.

I'm a fan of the late Thomas Kincade. His painting, *Sunday Evening Sleigh Ride*, presents a setting that features elements characteristic of all three of the relationships under consideration.

In that painting, there is a church whose lights shine through the windows, along with an open door, both resisting the approach of darkness. There is enough light shining through from the inside that one can see the lake behind the church and the reflection of the surrounding snow-capped trees. In front of the church some folks are gathering for evening worship and another family is approaching in a horse-drawn sleigh. Surrounding the church are the homes of people in the community.

For me, the scene captures the beautiful blend of our relationship with *God, others and nature*. Each component complements the other. I behold the painting and feel touched at my deepest level. When I have left the scene, the scene has not left me. It stays, continuously releasing a measure of meaning. The experience calls to memory the words of Maltbie D. Babcock's hymn:

This is my Father's world, and to my listening ears all nature rings and round me sings the music of the spheres. This is my Father's world, I rest me in the thought of rocks and trees, of skies and seas; God's hands the wonders wrought.

This is my Father's world, the birds their carols raise, the morning life, the flowers bright, declare their Maker's praise. Our God has made this world and shines in all that's fair; in rustling grass I hears God pass, who speaks to me everywhere.

Our God has made this world; oh, let us not forget that though the wrong seems oft so strong, God is ruler yet. God trusts us with this world, to keep it clean and fair. All earth and trees, the skies and seas, God's creatures everywhere. (Chalice Hymnal, 1995).

The inextricable connection among the three categories of relationships reflects a remarkable design. To experience their interwoven character inspires and expands us while it enables us to open ourselves to the flood of meaning that is available for our enrichment when we extract their content.

To do the work of mining one must be equipped with the appropriate tools. Let us now move to identify those.

As we have affirmed, each of the relational categories under consideration constitutes a rich vein of meaning waiting to be extracted and utilized. Obviously, in this mining metaphor, by *tool* we are not referring to tangible mining instruments such as picks and shovels, and loading carts, but to experiences that serve as effective instruments for getting inside each vein. We are looking for dynamic words capable of empowering us for effective engagement with these relationships.

As your will see, while I have chosen a particular word to represent a tool for mining, you may find that a particular word *tool* may work for one or more of the other categories. I do not intend them to be interchangeable, however. Each has been chosen because of its particular effectiveness in mining the relational category for which it is chosen.

The Tool for Mining Our Relationship with God: The primary criteria for the word tool by which we are able to mine this particular relationship are these: It must reflect the primacy of God and, at the same time, the capability of human beings to utilize it. These criteria come from the heart of the Judeo-Christian faith in which the primacy of God, the Creator, stands tallest in relationship with all else. On the other hand, the Supreme earnestly desires a relationship with all creation, particularly with human beings, and, therefore, only asks of us that of which we are capable.

Obviously, any word tool that does not consider God's supremacy, will not be adequate and will fail. Our word choice here, therefore, is to be chosen with considerable care.

The word I have chosen is TRUST. Trust is a powerful tool for mining the vein of meaning made available in our relationship with God.

You may be surprised that I did not choose the word faith which seems more popular in our culture. I suggest that, while this word may be more popular, the meaning attached to it these days may lead us away from its root meaning as used in the Bible. In contemporary society, the word faith may direct our thoughts toward identifying particular religious traditions like, Catholic, Protestant, Buddhism, Hinduism, etc. For example, in a social gathering someone may ask, "What faith are you?" expecting to hear about the religious tradition in which one stands.

In my thinking, an even more damaging digression the word faith may prompt lies in the direction of that to which we give intellectual affirmation; reflected in such statements as "I believe in God" or "I believe in Hell or Heaven" as though faith is a matter of the head and, therefore, essentially has to do with the doctrines one believes. With doctrinal content emphasized, one is led to conclude that their relationship with God is basically a matter of having correct intellectual beliefs about God.

Therefore, in light of the inadequate directions contemporary understandings of faith takes us, I prefer the word *trust*. This is not to suggest that the things we believe about God are unimportant. It is, however, to suggest that trust goes to a deeper level than what we may believe about different things. In the New Testament, the Greek word for it is *pistis*, and although it is translated in many versions of Scripture as faith, it is faith understood as a trust in God so significant that one is willing to leap into the arms of God with deep assurance that the relationship is one that can be depended upon. For example, that trust which comes through when the writer of Psalm 23 declares, " *The Lord is my shepherd....(and)...I walk through the valley of the shadow of death, I fear no evil for thou art with me....*"

Think of this, one can have beliefs about God which may not contain the element of trust. If we settle with beliefs about God, we may never reach the point of trusting God. In this context, as I earlier suggested, faith becomes a matter of the intellect, and not of the heart. While I believe the intellect to be crucial in the life of faith, I also believe that its foundation is trust.

On June 14, 2012, Nick Wallenda walked across a wire stretched across Niagara Falls. Millions of us were captivated by the scene as television cameras focused upon the stand from which he began his journey across. Though I was confident he could pull it off I was anxious about the possibility of some little slip that could result in a dangerous fall.

With considerable respect for Wallenda's achievement that night, in our imagination, let's play a little with that Niagara Falls scene. Imagine that we are on the stand with him as he prepares to begin his journey across the wire. He turns to us and asks, "Do you guys think I can do this?" I can see us nodding in the affirmative, perhaps thinking, "His reputation as a tight rope walker is impeccable...no doubt, he can do this." Now imagine him turning directly to you and asking. "Do you think I can do this?" Momentarily shocked by his direct approach, you respond with confidence, "Yes, Mr. Wallenda, I do!"

Now, let your imagination take another step in which you see him take a wheelbarrow from his assembled tools, then turn to look you directly in the eye, and ask, "Do you believe I can do this, rolling this wheelbarrow in front of me?" "Well...yes!" you exclaim, whereupon he offers you this challenge: "Then, get in!" At that point your belief about his successful execution of the walk is put to the test and the test is this: Do you move beyond belief to trust?

In this imaginary appendage to the actual story, the act of getting into the wheelbarrow moves us beyond mere verbal affirmation to a point of action which grows out of active trust. In other words, as we cast ourselves upon God in a leap of faith, we move beyond talking the talk to walking the walk.

Trust is a quality that transcends beliefs about God and empowers us to place ourselves in God's hands with strong confidence in God's sovereign love.

Now, reflect for a moment, on what a powerful tool trust becomes as we develop our relationship with God. Such trust enables us to dig deeply into the vein of meaning that God has planted there for us. I believe that when one trusts God, she or he cannot miss the oasis of meaning that is there in the middle of the desert of meaninglessness and lack of purpose.

When all literature is considered, Psalm 23, from the hand of one who experienced this quality of trust is one of the finest examples of how trust enhances life. With fresh hearing, listen to it from the King James Version:

The Lord is my shepherd, I shall not want; he maketh me lie down in green pastures. He leadeth me beside still waters; he restoreth my soul. He leadeth me in paths of righteousness for his name's sake. Even though I walk through the valley of the shadow of death, I fear no evil, for thou art with me, thy rod and thy staff, they comfort me. Thou preparest a table before me in the presence of mine enemies, thou annointest my head with oil, my cup overflows. Surely goodness and mercy shall follow me all the days of my life, and I will dwell in the house of the Lord forever.

I suggest you read it again, slowly and reflectively. As you are able, consider yourself as the psalmist who is writing it. Let his words become yours. Sense the trust in the heart of the author? Does your reading aid you in realizing that the trust of the psalmist is steady in both the good times (those times of relaxation and nourishment of soul and body) and the bad (those times in which he is surrounded by threat)?

Now think of other examples of such trust: Moses, St. Paul, Joan of Arc, Martin Luther, Pope John Paul, Mother Theresa, and Martin Luther King, Jr. In expanding the list to reflect upon our own acquaintances, we can name scores of persons in whom this quality of trust is detected.

Hymns sung by worshiping congregations continue to be remarkable expressions of trust in God. Consider, for example, "O God Our Help in Ages Past," penned by Isaac Watts in 1719:

O God, our help in ages past, our hope for years to come,
Our shelter from the stormy blast and our eternal home.

Under the shadow of thy throne still may we dwell secure;
Sufficient is thine arm alone and our defense is sure.

O God, our help in ages past, our hope for years to come,
Be though our guide while life shall last, and our eternal
home (vss. 1, 2 and 6) Chalice Hymnal, 1995

Significantly, whether in Scripture, hymns, or other avenues, persons of faith have expressed and continue to express trust in God, even while affirming God's profound mystery. It's as though we are confessing that even without a complete understanding of God, we experience enough to trust completely God's love for us.

Trusting God has opened floodgates through which meaning continues to flow into our lives. As the old hymn admonishes, I regularly, "count my blessings" and, as best I can, "name them one by one" in order "to see what God has done."

God continues to be remarkably faithful to you and me! Our experience of trusting God's presence and deliverance in face of threatening challenges has proved to be a strong incentive for our growth and development, propelling us forward with confidence that God's deliverance is not a one-time thing but a perpetual and eternal reality.

Trusting God is the tool with which millions of us continue to mine the vein of meaning offered by our relationship with God. It enables us to dig into, discover, assimilate, and share the rich meaning planted there. All who experience it find the abundant life of which Jesus spoke so eloquently.

Let's now turn to a consideration of the tool which enables us to mine meaning from our relationship with others. I've given a lot of thought to identifying a tool for mining this vein. During that process I have been aware that whatever word we use, it must be strong enough to pry us loose from those things which hold us from others, powerful blocking forces to healthy relationships. Consider, for example, the strong influence of self-preoccupation which fills us with so much concern about our own security that we have little time or inclination to reach out to others. Add to that our tendency to exert ourselves in accumulating stuff with what, at times, appears to be an insatiable appetite. Such accumulation anxiety has the effect of turning us into human whirlpools that attempt to suck everything into themselves.

In times of crisis, the tendency seems to strengthen, intensified by a spirit of panic, and pressing us beyond simple preoccupation to the point at which we see ourselves in a contesting struggle with others for life's resources. Under such circumstances, others may be perceived as adversaries to be overcome as a means of establishing our own security.

Self-preoccupation is not the only force blocking our positive, life-giving relationship with others. Another is *indifference.* While this state of mind may seem less intense than that of self-preoccupation, it is fully capable of blocking us from a relationship with others. It renders us capable of blinding ourselves to our need for others and their need for us, allowing ourselves to become anesthetized to their existence. Of course, at the intellectual level we may acknowledge the fact that others are here on the planet with us, but simply choose to ignore them. In absence of an alive social sensitivity, we simply grow numb of their presence.

My point is that, in light of these haunting realities, whatever tool we use to mine the vein of our relationship with others must equip us with a process of liberation from the resisting forces of self-preoccupation and social indifference.

It is imperative that such a tool is able to create the kind of excitement about the reality of others that we are motivated to move toward them in such a way that we involve ourselves with them, both to contribute to them and to allow them to contribute to us.

What kind of tool is able to propel us toward others with such keep anticipation about the positive things that can happen when we are connected with them? My consideration of that issue has given me the word *compassion*.

Think about the strength of that word. It comes from two Latin words: *com* (with) and *pati* (to suffer); suggesting that compassion is a force that enables us to be both empathetic and sympathetic with others to the point, if necessary, we stretch ourselves on their behalf.

In reporting an incident in Jesus' life, Matthew's Gospel gives us an example of compassion in action:

Then Jesus went about all the cities and villages teaching in their synagogues, and proclaiming the good news of the kingdom, and curing every disease and sickness. When he saw the crowds, he had compassion for them, because they were harassed and helpless, like sheep without a shepherd (9:35—NRSV).

Such compassion, whether in Jesus' life or our own, breaks the shackles of self-preoccupation and indifference, thereby propelling us forward into redemptive involvement with others.

Lying behind the energizing force of compassion is a conviction that others—all others—have value and dignity, and that becoming a person for others not only completes them, but also completes us. Sometime, those to whom we reach may need us to help lift them out of the jaws of hunger or some other human predicament. At other times, of course, people around us may appear not to be stuck in some dilemma. Whatever circumstances we may discover among those around us, our sensitivity to them becomes an important pathway into an experience of community versus compulsive isolation.

Consider how friendships have enriched your life. In the experience of being among friends and celebrating life our lives develop sparkle. But, even when relationships may not have moved to the high level of friendship, the experience of seeing others as brothers and sisters in the human family enables us to recognize the dignity and value of everyone which, in turn, enables us to breathe the rich air of living affirmatively toward others.

To me, one of the most meaningful stories in the Bible is the one in which Jesus is responding to the inquirer who, realizing the importance of reaching out to neighbors, asks, "Who is my neighbor?" In good rabbinical style, Jesus responds with a story:

There was once a man who was going down from Jerusalem to Jericho when robbers attacked him, stripped him, and beat him up, leaving him half dead. It so happened that a priest was going down that road; but when he saw the man, he walked by on the other side. In the same way a Levite also came there, went over and looked at him, and then walked on by on the other side. But a Samaritan who was traveling this way came upon the man, and when he saw him, his heart was filled with pity. He went over to him, poured oil and wine on his wounds and bandaged them, then he put the man on his own animal and took him to an inn, where he took care of him. The next day he took out two silver coins and gave them to the innkeeper, "Take care of him," he told the innkeeper, "...and when I come back this way, I will pay you whatever else you spend on him." And then, Jesus concluded, "In your opinion, which one of these acted like a neighbor toward the man attacked by the robbers? The teacher of the Law answered, "The one who was kind to him." Jesus replied, "You go, then, and do the same" (Luke 10:30-37—TEV).

Do you see it? No matter who we are—privileged or unprivileged, we unlock abundant meaning when we move compassionately toward others. Such a move yields meaning not only for those to whom we respond but , also, for ourselves. Imagine the thankful spirit of the victim who, as he healed, thought of how fortunate he was to have been rescued by the Samaritan. Now, stretch your imagination to see what was going on in the Samaritan's spirit as he rode away from leaving the victim in the care of the innkeeper. Can you sense the joy in his heart that grows out of his compassion to give new dimensions of meaning to his life?

A precious memory serves me here: When my younger brother and I were children, we accompanied our parents on regular visits to our paternal grandmother. Following a sumptuous evening meal, we would retire to the living room to sing hymns from grandmother's old paperback song books. I am now aware that some of my deepest impressions about faithful living came from the insights of those old hymns. Most of them were written in four-part harmony—soprano, alto, bass, and tenor. Mom, Dad, Eddie and I each took a part and off we would go into harmony land.

One of the hymns, entitled, "A Beautiful Life" declared:

Each day I'll do a golden deed by helping those who are in need.

My life on earth is but a span, and so I'll do the best I can.

Refrain: Life's evening sun is sinking low, a few more days and I must go

To meet the deeds that I have done, where there will be no setting sun.

To be a child of God each day, my light must shine along the way.

I'll sing God's praise while the ages roll and strive to help some troubled soul. (Source Unknown)

That song's impression upon me was deep and enduring. Along with so many other experiences during those formative days, I became sensitized to the concept of human community and to my responsibility for valuing others; especially those who are victims of life. Though I did not realize it at the time, hindsight teaches me that I was drinking from a very rich fountain whose waters would continue to flood my life with abundant meaning and clear purpose.

A compassionate person is able to transcend the combative and aloof styles dictated by self-preoccupation and indifference, and soar to the style so popularized by Jesus, that of servant. The spirit that enables such an experience is caught in a persuasive hymn written by Richard Gillard in 1977, "Sister, Let Me Be Your servant":

Sister, let me be your servant, brother, let me walk with you; Pray that I may have the grace to let you be my servant too.

We are pilgrims on a journey, fellow trav'lers on the road.

We are here to help each other walk the mile and bear the load.

I will weep when you are weeping, when you laugh I'll laugh with you.

I will share your joy and sorrow till we've seen this journey thro'.

When we sing to God In heaven, we shall find each harmony

Born of all we've known together of great love and agony.

Brother, let me be your servant, sister, let me walk with you,

Pray that I may have the grace to let you be my servant too

(Chalice Hymnal).

The compassionate lifestyle dramatically blesses us and others. As *trust* is the word tool by which we mine the vein of our relationship with God, *compassion* is the one we use to extract the meaning for life that comes from mining the vein of our relationship with others.

We turn now to a tool with which to mine the rich vein of our relationship with nature. The word tool used here must have the power to overcome the prevailing state of desensitization to nature. As indicated earlier, Richard Louv acknowledges this state, calling it "natural deficit disorder." Connecting it directly to our desensitization and its consequence, he writes:

> *By its broader interpretation, nature deficit disorder is an atrophied awareness, a diminished ability to find meaning in the life that surrounds us, whatever form it takes. This shrinkage of our lives has a direct impact on our physical, mental, and societal health.* 1

As I hear this, the image that comes to my mind is that of a door closed to the wonder and fulfillment surrounding us in nature, blocking our senses to her life-giving gifts. It is a situation of serious closedness prompting this declaration from Diane Ackerman:

> *People think of the mind as being located in the head, but the latest findings in physiology suggest that the mind doesn't really dwell in the brain, but travels the whole body on caravans of enzymes, busily making sense of the compound wonders we catalogue as touch, taste, smell, hearing, vision.* 2

From Ackerman's observation, I take our desensitization to nature to indicate the closing of our very being to nature's fulfillment potential.

John Buchannan strengthens Ackerman's point. Earlier, I referenced his *Universal Feeling* in which , from his interfacing of the perspectives of process philosopher, Alfred North Whitehead, and transpersonal psychologist, Stanislav Grof, he concludes that human experience is richer when it is not limited to that which comes from mere rationalism or materialism.

For example, with regard to nature, Buchannan is convinced that we must not limit our relationship with nature to our five senses. He calls us to utilize extrasensory perception as a way of expanding our capacity for receiving what nature has to offer.

David Ray Griffin, Professor of Religion and Philosophy at Clairmont School of Theology, amplifies Buchannan's point. In his *Parapsychology, Philosophy, and Spirituality*, Griffin calls for new paradigms that will encourage our reliance upon extrasensory perception to enhance our ability to access realities in and around us. He wants us to realize that our resistance to new paradigms is encouraged by modernity which views extrasensory options with deep suspicion. In light of this, Griffin makes a case for moving beyond those limitations toward more realistic, liberating, and sustainable insights:

Modernity, besides having turned out to be socially and ecologically unsustainable, has also been intellectually and spiritually unsatisfactory. The late modern worldview, with its atheism, materialism, and resulting nihilism, has generally been recognized as spiritually unsatisfactory from the outset— even by its proponents, who have said that we had to embrace it nevertheless, putting loyalty to truth above the will to believe. In our time, however, both scientific developments and philosophical considerations have led to the growing realization that this late modern worldview is also inadequate intellectually. So now, the ferment to move from the modern to a post-modern world is being fueled by intellectual and spiritual energies as well as by social, political, economic, and ecological pressures. 3

Dr. Griffin believes that this movement from the limitations of modernity to the liberating effects of post modernity enables us to affirm and utilize capacities which have been denied or discouraged. Openness to paranormal phenomena is, therefore, encouraged in order better to access the fulfilling potentialities of our relationship with nature.

> According to Griffin, there are three major types of these phenomena: (1) extrasensory perception, primarily telepathy and clairvoyance, (2) psychokinesis in which, by the psyche, one is able to produce effects beyond the body without using one's body, and (3) that which Griffin calls other experiences, *"...such as messages from mediums and near-death-out of body experiences which are suggestive of the existence psyches apart from their physical bodies."* 4

> *The credibility of these paranormal phenomena has been clinically established and are being utilized to expand our access to sources of meaning that have traditionally been discouraged. Dr. Griffin's encouragement with the expansion can be sensed when he declares, "...the human mind as power of its own beyond that of the brain-power with which it can directly perceive and directly act on things beyond the body...."* 5

Elaborating that point, he writes:

> *The fact that extrasensory perception occurs and cannot be understood in terms of physical fields suggests that we have a receptive center other than the brain and its sensory organs. The fact that psychokinesis occurs and cannot be understood in terms of brain waves suggests a center of activity that transcends the brain. Given the reality of the*

*soul as distinct from the brain, our presupposition that
have a degree of self-determining freedom can be taken at
face value.* 6

I believe the fresh directions emerging from the insights of both
Buchannan and Griffin have rich implications in our search for a
word tool with which to mine the rich vein of our relationship with
nature. One of the more prominent of those fresh directions is the
desire to become liberated from exclusive dependence upon our
five senses as a way of apprehending and being apprehended by
the wide world of nature.

This liberation, I believe, will enable us to develop a more
promising posture toward experiencing nature's potential for
blessing us and being blessed by us. It is this posture that suggests
to me the word tool, *openness*.

Louv helps us to see that our nature deficit disorder has grown
out of our closure to nature, a closure buttressed by limiting our
access to a relationship with her through our five senses. When we
add to that limitation the alienating issues of technology and urban
living, we begin to see the strength of the closed door standing
between us and the gifts nature offers.

Given these circumstances, how do we begin to engage—or
reengage—with nature? How can we open the closed door that
prevents such engagement?

I believe it begins with our preparation. The analogy of a closed
door suggests that some oiling of the hinges, stiff and rusty
from disuse, needs to occur. I suspect that many of us have been
challenged by such an obstacle as we have attempted to enter an
old house or cellar whose door hinges have not been exercised for
a long period.

Perhaps the analogy speaks to the condition of the hearts of those who have become victims of a nature deficit disorder. In my childhood and early adolescence, I always felt intimate with my natural surroundings. As I grew into young adulthood I began to sense that I was moving away from my previous relationship with nature as I became more focused upon the issues of studying for my degrees, launching a career, living in the city, providing for my family, etc. When prompted, my brain acknowledged the existence of nature, but I had become disengaged with her. My sensitivity had grown dull. As a result, my awareness was blurred. Nevertheless, something within had triggered the memory of my earlier stimulating engagement with her. Eventually, this memory grew into a longing to return to the banquet she offers. My desire to re-engage became strong but the hinges of the separating door were rusty. Lubrication was needed. For me, that came in the form of stimulating my desire and appetite for interaction with nature and more intentional and sustained exposure to her.

That work of preparation is not easy. When we have limited ourselves to a steady diet of routines and performances of duties, along with technology's temptation toward preoccupation with gadgets, adjustments leading to re-engagement with nature are not easily achieved.

In addition to the rusty hinge challenge, another becomes the issue of how to re-engage with nature in such a way that we do not abandon the responsibilities to our working careers, planning for our families, supporting just causes for better communities and environment, etc. In short, how do we re-engage with nature through a balanced approach that brings fresh vitality and meaning to all we do? Louv's term for such balanced re-engagement is the development of a "hybrid mind" that is able to integrate our experience with nature and our duty to family and career.

With such strategy for re-engaging with nature, eventually, we break through. The door opens and we walk through to the bounty nature has prepared for all who come to her. Entering, we become aware of the quality of the experiences awaiting us as we experience a growing realization that nature—including ourselves as a part of it—has the capacity both to initiate and respond, we find ourselves giving and receiving.

Let me illustrate the initiating movement toward nature by sharing an experience with Sand Hill Cranes so prominent in our part of Southwest Florida. Several years ago, while visiting the construction of our new house, a few of these cranes appeared from around the corner of construction and walked with a few feet of me, as though awaiting an invitation to review the site with me. There they were, tall, magnificent, and curious. The red feathers of their head gave way to a bridge of white, connecting to a torso of brownish gray. Stabilizing their torso were two perfectly strong, stilt-like, hinged legs designed for wading, running and flying.

Speaking softly, to assure them that I intended no harm, I walked slowly toward, then, among them. While maintaining a safe distance, they engaged me, responding positively to my voice and my gestures. Eventually, appearing more relaxed, they began walking directly up to me, making low, chuckling sounds. Face to face, we fellowshipped in a way that was very satisfying to me, and apparently to them as well. They followed me into and through the partially constructed building giving me a feeling of conducting a most unusual tour.

On a more recent occasion, while playing golf, I drove the golf cart to the area where my ball had landed. Assembled there were two Sand Hill parents along with their chick . With their beaks, the parents were piercing the soil to capture small worms and bugs which, in turn, they passed on to the chick eager to receive the morsels. Being very protective, the parents moved into a position between my cart and their chick and stood erect, intensely staring at me, an action which I interpreted as a sign for me to come no closer. I stopped the cart and softly intoned, "I am not going to harm your chick. I, too, treasure it." Lingering there for a moment, I continued to speak and gesture calmly as I slowly drove away feeling invigorated by what I perceived to be a meaningful interaction, enhanced by mutual respect and trust between the birds and me. Whenever I see this species I always initiate friendly words and actions that continue to build my relationship with them.

My engagement with different species, both animate and inanimate, has brought me to a point at which I find my relationship with nature being restored. Because the relationship is dynamic, I feel I have reentered a process with nature that will continue to bless me with delight and compel me to respect and advocate both her development and protection.

My exposure to nature sometimes puts me in the role of receiver as she initiates toward me. On a recent evening I went into a field away from the neighborhood lights. Lying on my back in the grass and fixing my eyes upon the sky, I was amazed by the number and brilliance of its heavenly bodies. Initially, there seemed to be little movement among them, as though they were awaiting a starting signal; then, as though prompted by some mysterious force, the heavens began to perform with a shooting star slicing across the sky like a cosmic tracer bullet. Its action seemed to awaken the entire scene as the stationary ones took on added brilliance and began to twinkle. This awesome view stirred my imagination, reminding me that the view was only a small part of an infinitesimally larger scene not only within our immediate solar system but also in incalculable larger ones.

The longer I lay there, entertained by the starlit sky, the more I felt blessed by the significant value she seemed to place upon me. Departing the scene, I had a sense of fulfillment and completion that comes with a pleasant experience of distant inanimate beings that seemed to acknowledge and care for me.

These experiences are single examples of multiple ones available to the person who cultivates a relationship with nature. Moreover, they illustrate how both the person and the natural phenomena to which she or he relates, initiate and receive the energy of that interaction.

In order to sustain this dynamic relationship with nature, I find it important for me to monitor and sharpen my sensitivity to natural surroundings. Earlier, I told you of my Yorkie, Moose. I've learned much from him during the seven years of a part of our family. During a recent evening when my spouse and I sat watching a television program, I rose to get a glass of my favorite, peach tea. At the time, Moose lay with her on the couch, apparently asleep. But as I rose and walked across the room, though he remained in his relaxed position, I could see his ears, funneling and adjusting to follow the progression of my movement. With my drink in hand, I returned to my chair with those funneled ears following me all the way. Suddenly, I realized afresh that Moose's constant attention to where I am and what I am doing tells me that he cares immensely for me. Deeply moved by that, I said to him, "I know what's going with you Moose man. You've just got to be in touch with me at all times, and I love you for that!"

This experience addresses the constancy and sensitivity needed toward our natural surroundings if we are to experience their richness. Our relationship with nature calls for more than an occasional change of pace to which we resort when there is nothing else to do. I find that practicing the presence and vitality of nature when I am in my study, on the golf course, at worship, or in a conference is helpful. As constant sensitivity to God and to others provides an open door for interaction, so does such constancy with nature. We are at our best when such constancy in each of our three relational categories becomes a way of living, thinking, and experiencing life. Such sensitivity defines us. These relationships are not appendages to life, but the air we breathe and the avenues through which we journey with meaning.

CONCLUSION

Believing that meaning for our lives comes from our relationship with God, others, and nature, I have imagined those relationships as veritable mines packed with rich veins of meaning awaiting our discovery and utilization. Moreover, I have expressed my conviction that each relationship's life-giving meaning is magnified into something even more profound when we connect all three and experience the chemistry of their complementarity. With equal conviction, I have attempted to highlight a challenge which acts as a blockade to gaining access to the meaning these relationships offer, namely, our tendency to diminish the scope of each of the relational categories resulting in dwarfed concepts of God, bias and discrimination in the human community, and diminution of the dynamic character of nature, in face of which I believe we must stretch ourselves beyond such limitations and opt for broader, more inclusive perceptions and experiences.

An additional step I have taken is the identification of tools designed to aid us in this stretching and broadening effort, tools that serve as effective instruments in mining deeply for meaning in each of the relational categories---*trust* in relating to God, *compassion* in relating to others, and *openness* in relating to nature.

Increasingly, it seems, we are becoming convinced that life is destined to have meaning. In our own time this experience has spawned what may be an unprecedented search for it. I believe that this heightened search is reflected in a general yearning for an experienced level of meaning that our steady diet of materialism, technological gadgetry, and stifling routines is unable to give us. All around us—in our homes, workplaces, coffee shops, theatres, churches, hospitals, sports venues, and vacation travel—we are seeking to discover and unlock what we suspect is a reservoir of meaning which has the capacity to enrich life considerably.

Now, in my concluding statements, I want to zoom in on a description of that meaningful state of being. It has a name: *Shalom*, a Hebrew word used widely in Judeo-Christian faith communities as both a hello and a farewell greeting. But as in the case of many Hebrew words, it has deeper dimensions that extend beyond peace greetings and fond farewells. It's root meaning triggers our hope as it points to an experience of being complete, whole, well-rounded and fulfilled. It suggests such qualities as health in body, mind and spirit, safety, tranquility, prosperity, perfection, rest, and harmony, all of which defy the debilitating effects of anxiety, agitation, discord, and meaninglessness.

A primary characteristic of a *shalom state of being* is its ability to experience these gifts even in the midst of tumultuous circumstances. As *homeostasis* provides our bodies with chemical balance which allows us a steady temperature in the presence of cold or heat, *shalom* offers us emotional and spiritual balance in face of those forces that have the potential to knock us down.

It's a beautiful thing when our key relationships are healthy and we experience a sense of harmony and well-being that sustains us even when surrounded by the tumultuous world.

This *shalom* state of being emerges from a strong sense of belonging both to the Creator and to all things created. In it, we are given the ability to celebrate this magnificent fruit of our relationships and to delight in its gifts of respecting and being respected, loving and being loved. Encouragement floods us with anticipation of a future in which our own experience expands beyond us, into a wider portion of creation, generating unity and harmony among peoples and throughout nature.

Therefore, it is good for us to remember that this blessed state of being for any individual is no an end in itself. At its heart, it is always in motion, constantly pointing us beyond the present moment toward the future while fulfilling us with s ense of compassion for those around us who continue to drown in a sea of meaninglessness.

Shalom's hope propels us forward in confidence that the future is the arena in which we shall see not only its expansion beyond ourselves, but also within ourselves as we continue to experience new dimensions in our experience with God, one another, and the ever-expanding world of nature.

In the future—as in the past and present—we keep our eyes peeled on the goal to reduce the gap between the Creator and creation, the hostility among human beings, and the abuse of nature. Gaps, hostility, and abuse are forces which continue to stand in the way of everything coming together in wholeness or, in Biblical terms, the forces that resist God's process of *"reconciling all things to himself"* (2 Corinthians 5:18).

This vision of hope, so central to the Biblical faith is called eschatological faith which has at its center a conviction that all creation is being led toward its intended destiny, reflected in such concepts as fulfillment, purpose, peace, and wholeness. This posture of hope and trust seems to be the conceptual context out of which Jesus speaks in that which we know as The Lord's Prayer in which he prays, *"…Thy kingdom come, Thy will be done on earth as it is in heaven."* That prayer is full of expectation that all creation is being renewed (restored) from its present state of fragmentation and disharmony into a perfect state of wholeness and harmony.

As it did with Jesus, a *shalom* state of being pulls us into the future in the hope that, ultimately, all people and things will experience its fulfillment in the Kingdom of God. Though that reality is a work in progress, not yet fully realized, persons of faith have a strong sense of its reality in the present; prompting Jesus to declare, *"I am telling you the truth: those who hear my words and believe in him who sent me have (already) eternal life"* (John 5:24—TEV) and *"We know that we have left death and come over into life, we know it because we love one another"* (John 3:14—TEV).

Reflecting upon such passages, Biblical theologians, beginning with C.H. Dodd, have long held that in persons of faith there is a *realized eschatology*, i.e., a present experience of a promised future.

For me, the meaning of life is significantly enhanced in an experience of that "realized" eschatological hope: that everyone and everything is in process of being reconciled to the Creator with such magnificence and power that we, those folk around us, and nature—all things—are in the process of being set free to live in peace, unity, harmony, and with a deep sense of meaning and purpose.

That vision raises an important issue for us. Through the years I have encountered people who seem convinced that those of us in the community of the reconciled will witness a time when God's vengeance will get even with those who resist reconciliation. Increasingly, however, it becomes clearer to me that the community of the reconciled and the God of reconciliation seek not to destroy those who resist them, but to liberate them from their bondage and integrate them into their divine destiny in such a way that, ultimately, there are no winners and losers, only winners. 1

Persuasively, theologian Jurgen Moltmann speaks to this dramatic eschatological process of reconciliation by describing the destiny of "executioners" and their "victims."

> *The message of the new righteousness which eschatological faith brings into the world says that in face the executioners will not finally triumph over their victims. It also says that in the end the victims will not triumph over the executioners. The one (Jesus) will triumph who first died for the victims and then also for the executioners, and in so doing revealed a new righteousness which breaks the vicious circles of hate and vengeance which, from the victims and executioners, creates a new humanity.* 2

EPILOGUE

It seems to be such a simple thing to identify our relationships with God, one another, and nature as rich sources of meaning. But things are not always as they seem, for there are millions who, for various reasons, have not experienced their richness.

Among those millions are those of us who have become obsessed with our busy routines that tend to dwarf the human spirit, routines that limit an experience of the vast world both within and beyond the human soul, and restrict our vision of history and the future. In short, such routines have a way of "thingifying" us by stealing from us, those dimensions which make us human.

Those of us who allow ourselves to become dull, insensitive, and apathetic with regard to our relationships, condemn ourselves to a dungeon of loneliness where living requires less imagination, creativity, and exertion of energy required in building relationships. Life in such a cocoon-like isolation seems more comfortable.

And there are those of us who are victims, not of monotonous routines or apathy, but something perhaps more destructive—we are filled with a troubled spirit that seems determined to express anger and create disharmony. Others, even God, are perceived as adversaries with whom we are compelled to be in tension.

The results of living outside these life-giving relationships are not pretty. Typically, they yield such life-complicating fruits as *nihilism* (whose perspective holds that there is no point or meaning to life) or *cynicism* (in which life is perceived as a Gordian knot whose complexity amounts to hopeless deadlock) or *triumphalism* (in which relationships are perceived as contests which one must win and the other lose).

Those options leave little, if any room for the positive, meaning-filled and life-giving relationships described in this book.

An experience of a healthy relationship with God, one another, and nature introduces us to a much different world. It is to that more positive world, discovered on the wings of healthy relationships with God, one another, and nature, I have endeavored to invite you. Thank you very much for taking the time to read *Mining for Meaning*. My hope is that each of us will enter into the relationships it outlines in such a way that we may not only find abundant meaning and purpose for ourselves but for others who, seeing our fulfillment, are moved to seek it for themselves.

END

NOTES

Preface:

1 Thomas Merton, *No Man Is an Island*, (Boston: Shambala Press, 2005), xi

2 Victor E. Frankl, *Man's Search for Meaning*, (New York: Basic Books, 2000)pp. 84,85

3 Diana Butler Bass, *Christianity After Religion* (New York: Harper One, 2012) p. 190

4 Ibid, p. 194

5 Ibid, pp 307,310 in reference to writing by Herbert Mead

Chapter One:

1 Philip Yancey, *What's So Amazing about grace*, (Grand Rapids: Zondervan, 1997) p. 45

2 Henri Nouwen, *The Return of the Prodigal Son*, (New York: Doubleday, 1994) pp.129-130

3 John Shelby Spong, *A New Christianity for a New World*, (San Francisco: Harper San Francisco, 2001) p. 21

4 Ibid, p.54

5 Ibid, xvii

6 Victor Frankl, *Man's Search for Meaning* (New York: Pocket Books, 1984) p. 17

7 Op. Cit, Spong, p. 58

Chapter Two:

1 Op. Cit., Merton, pp. 9,10

2 Ibid, pp. 1-12

3 In his, *A Time to Embrace Same-Gender Relationships in Religion, Law, and Politics, (Grand Rapids/Cambridge, U.K., 2006)* systematic theologian William Stacy Johnson of Princeton University outlines seven points of view reflected among people of faith these days, ranging from prohibition of all such relationships to affirmation. I reference them here to illustrate that there is no monolithic Christian position, but a plurality of positions within the Christian community: *Prohibition* (does not approve of and would bar same-gender unions), *Toleration* (does not approve but would not persecute gay and lesbian people), *Accommodation* (does not approve ordinarily, but would allow for exceptions on a 'lesser of evils" rationale), *Legitimation* (wants to include gays and lesbians in the community and wants to prevent them from being singled out and condemned unfairly), *Celebration* (believes same-gender unions should no longer be scorned but affirmed as good, *Liberation* (perceives societal attitudes concerning gays and lesbians as being caught up in wider injustices which need to be remedied), *Consecration* (argues for the full religious blessing of

same-gender unions).

4 Op. Cit., Yancey, p.91

5 Helmut Thielicke, *The Waiting Father*, (San Francisco: Harper and Row, 1959) p. 81

Chapter Three:

1 Richard Louv, *The Nature Principle*, (New York: Workman Publishing) p. 253

2 Theodore Hichert, *Interpretation, as quote in The Christian Century*, January 11, 2012

3 Jurgen Moltmann, *The Future of Creation*, (Philadelphia: Fortress Press, 1979) p. 130

4 Op. Cit. Louv, p. 62

5 Ibid, Louv, p. 108

6 Seth Borenstein, *"Evidence Piles Up Showing Primates Act Similar to Us" as in the Sarasota Herald Tribune*, June 12, 2012

6 Ibid, *Sarasota Herald Tribune*

7 John H, Buchannan, *Universal Feeling*, (Ann Arbor: UMI Dissertation Services, 2007) pp7,8

8 Ibid, Buchannan's quote from *Stanislov Grof's, The Adventure of Self Discovery: Dimensions of Consciousness and New Perspectives in Psychotherapy and Inner Exploration* (Albany State University of New York Press)

9 Op. Cit. Buchannan, pp. 572,573

10 Op. Cit. Louv, p. 9

11 Ibid, pp 48,49

12 Ibid, p. 11

13 Diane Ackerman, *A Natural History of the Senses*, (New York: Random House, 1990) xix

14 David Ray Griffith, *Parapsychology, Philosophy, and Spirituality*, (New York: University of New York Press, 1997), pp 2,3

15 Ibid, p 4

16 Ibid, p 23

17 Ibid, p 272

Conclusion:

1 The issue of God's intention to reconcile all things, even those who resist reconciliation, is addressed beautifully in he work of two contemporary authors, Rob Bell, in his Love Wins, and Sharon Baker, in her Razing Hell: Rethinking Everything You've Been Taught about God's Wrath and Judgment

2 Jurgen Moltmann, *The Crucified God,* (London SCM, 1974), p 178